Graduating With Honor(s)

by

Daniel D. Deal

© 2004 by Daniel D. Deal. All rights reserved.

No part of this book may be reproduced, stored in a retrieval system, or transmitted by any means, electronic, mechanical, photocopying, recording, or otherwise, without written permission from the author.

First published by AuthorHouse 05/14/04

ISBN: 1-4184-7004-X (e-book)
ISBN: 1-4184-3193-1 (Paperback)

This book is printed on acid free paper.

GRADUATING WITH HONORS

Forward

I am grateful to God for the entire Deal family, and I am especially grateful to Matt. He continues to teach a young priest that the journey is never measured by the number of steps, but by the courage with which each step is taken.
   Rev. Michael L. Griffin

Author:
Dan Deal

DEDICATION

This book is dedicated to the people who have given me the courage to deal with the past year. The Tschetters, Father Mike and our Church community, the O'Gorman school staff, our network of friends, the Doyles, the Sawyers, the Johnson's, and the hundreds too many to mention.

Finally, this book is dedicated to my sons Chris and Andrew, for being true troopers through all of this, to Matt himself who is a courageous young man, and a true young man of character, and lastly to my wife of nearly twenty five years Janet. She is truly an angel on earth. Without her, none of us would have made it through this year.

In God's love.

Dan Deal

PROLOGE

Like the entire year, the days following graduation were incredible. The newspaper articles were exceptional and the television spots were beautiful. The highlight of the coverage for all of us was the pictures of Matt and Josh on the stage together. If there was one thing we wanted from all of this, it was to be able to thank Josh. The look on his face was incredible. The pure joy Josh had watching Matt walk across the stage was indescribable. He could not have looked more pleased had he won an Olympic gold medal. Everywhere we went for the next couple of months people stopped us to ask about Matt. One day he and I were at the wellness center lifting weights when a man came by. His jaw dropped and he stuttered, "you're the young man from the television interview. You are such an inspiration!" Matt just looked the man in the eye and thanked him. Matt knew this tragic illness had happened to him for a reason, because he was able to handle it.

Matt's progress following graduation has been slow but steady. Kim Wieking continues to bring him along slowly but surely. He has registered for classes at SDSU in Brookings and has enjoyed the summer playing video games with his brothers and our neighbors. To no surprise, as he has continued to progress, he spent his first weekend in a year away from home with who else, but the Tschetters. He is still expected to recover fully, and just the other day announced that the wheel chair will be history by the end of the month. I would expect it will be. Like his little brother Andrew says, it seems kind of strange coming down the hall and seeing this big body coming at you. It has been nearly a year since we saw him walk, and each time we see him we try not to take it for granted. Life is just too short to take anything for granted. If nothing else we have learned that during the past year.

Dan and Janet Deal

Forward: By Rev. Michael L. Griffin
December 2003
Christ the King Church
Sioux Falls, SD

Inspiring.

The word definitely comes to mind as I think back over the months of struggle Matt Deal and his family endured. Yet, I do not think of the word in the way many use it today.

For most, "inspiring" is the locker room address by the coach to fire up the team to play hard and to give all they have, and the team overcomes the odds and wins a stunning victory. Or perhaps they think of "inspiring" as the email they received from a friend that tells a wondrous tale, ending with people standing "with tears in their eyes," as a miracle occurs.

In most of these stories, the wonder and excitement comes at the end; the underdog wins or God makes an appearance when all is lost and brings about something wonderful. Perhaps this is the point of those kinds of stories, they are meant to encourage us.

Sure, they are inspiring but not in the same way the story of Matt and his family is inspiring. I think of the word in its oldest sense, to be inspired is to be "filled with the Spirit."

This is not a story in which the underdog simply beats the odds or a story where everything is made wonderful at the end; it is a part of a never-ending story. It is a journey. The inspiration comes from knowing that each step, each moment, is inspired: each is filled with the Spirit.

This is not a story where you have to wait until the end to discover the point; it is an invitation to walk with a special family on a journey. You are invited to discover, at each step along the way, some joyful, some excruciating, that the Spirit is there, always. It would be so easy to look at the struggle of this family and wonder where God is every step of the way. By walking with this wonderful family, you may even discover where Spirit is in your joys and sorrows, in your journey. You may discover that your life is inspiring as well.

I am grateful to God for the entire Deal family, and I am especially grateful to Matt. He continues to teach a young priest that the journey is never measured in the number of steps, but by the courage with which each step is taken.

Rev. Michael L. Griffin
December 2003

CHAPTER 1
EVERY STORY BEGINS SOMEWHERE

If I had known then, what I know now, I think I would have stayed in bed on this beautiful summer day in June of 2002. It was 5:30 am on a clear, crisp, sunny day in the western hills of South Dakota. I had risen early to get my morning run in before we traveled to Rapid City so our son, Chris, could play soccer at 8:00 am in the State Soccer Tournament. Chris had been asked to play with his cousin's soccer team. We had traveled to Spearfish a day early to spend the day with my wife's sister and her family. Betty and her husband Bob have lived at the top of Spearfish Canyon for nearly a decade. It is truly one of the most beautiful places on earth. Bob is a physician, Betty a nurse, and their house is straight out of Country Styles magazine complete with Comet their Black Labrador laying on the back door step.

As I ran down the hill I was amazed at how beautiful the Canyon was. I have been a runner for nearly three decades, and have always enjoyed running in the Canyon in all of its magnificence and glory. The beauty of this area has been documented many places, but perhaps best known are the scenic shots from the movie Dances with Wolves directed by Kevin Costner. After shooting the movie Costner apparently fell in love with this area, and has lived here off and on ever since. His parents supposedly live across the canyon from Betty and Bob. His brother operates one of the motels in Deadwood, a local historical town known for its gambling and gaming halls. Costner himself had proposed a major resort in this area a few years ago, but apparently the dream and the funding never matched.

As I began my run this morning the beauty of the Canyon again struck me. I tried to take in as much of the landscape as I could while still watching my feet beneath me. There was not a breath of wind in the air, and the temperature and humidity were nearly perfect. As I rolled along I set the timer on my watch. I wanted to run a thirty-minute stretch down the hill, and then return back up the hill in about the same time.

The run down was exceptionally steep. I reminded myself to take it easy; because once I turned around I would be coming back up this same route and the hill on the way back would be nearly impossible to run back up. As I got to the thirty-minute mark I was pleased because I had covered nearly three and one half miles. While not an exceptional pace, it did mean I would cover nearly seven miles in my hour run. This was a very fair effort for me. As I turned around to begin my trip back up the hill, I was reminded of the gunnery range at the top of the cliffs. In previous trips to the Canyon I recalled the shots of rifle fire startling me. They were always extremely loud and echoed for miles. This morning it was pleasant not to feel the shock of gun shots going off as I moved peacefully through the canyon.

As I rounded the corner near the two-mile mark I saw this figure coming down the hill from the opposite direction. It was a young man loping along bouncing up and down with each stride. The closer the figure got the more familiar the stride appeared. When we were within ten feet of each other I heard a voice call out "Hi Dad!" It was my oldest son Matt. Matt would be entering his senior year at O'Gorman High School in Sioux Falls next fall. He had always been an exceptional student and a so-so athlete. While he had always been involved in sports, his true passion was academics and more cerebral interests such as band. As we greeted each other he could see that I was surprised to see him. He said his cross-country coach, Doug Lindner, had told the team that he wanted them to run through the summer. He especially wanted the seniors to set an example for the rest of the team, so Matt figured since this was the first of June; it would be a good time to start his summer running program. He had heard me get up, so he had gotten out of bed, and followed behind me as I left that morning. Matt turned to join me, and as we began climbing back up the hill, it was obvious his pace was much quicker than mine. I struggled to keep up for a short time, but as we reached the steeper portion of the hill, his paced slowed as he began laboring due to the steep slope. Despite his lack of training and the seriousness of the terrain, Matt slowed, but was refusing to quit. He seemed committed to the fact that he would <u>run</u> up the hill. Matt's trip up the hill and his refusal to quit regardless of the pain was a trait that was going to come in handy in the months ahead.

That morning began what would be an exceptional summer for Matt and I, and an incredible year for our entire family. Though it was only June, we had already experienced a van wreck, a kitchen fire, and a broken leg by our youngest son Andrew. Not your ordinary every day fall and break your leg. Rather a slip through a hole in a merry go round, catch your ankle on a rail road spike kind of break that leaves a huge hole in your ankle, and shatters bone. Andrew had been riding a merry go round at an old country school during a school field trip. When Andrew's leg slipped through the hole in the merry go round his ankle caught on the spike and was impaled through to the bone. The result was an ambulance ride to the city, surgery, and the first eight weeks of his summer spent in a leg cast. This accident, the van wreck, and a fire to our kitchen were only a prelude to the events yet to come. While we thought that we had already had more than our share of bad luck, if we had known then what was to come in the months ahead we may have stayed on that hill in Spearfish Canyon forever.

Matt ran with me that morning, just as he ran with me every day for the rest of the summer. He was like a young puppy lapping at the heals of his master. I would come home from work each day and Matt would be sitting there with shoes in hand waiting for our daily run. During the summer Matt and I ran over 400 miles, and had the time of our lives! We raced to street corners, jumped curbs, dashed in between cars and were like young boys playing. We discussed politics, religion, family and nearly every other topic under the sun. Each day that we ran, Matt became more intense and competitive. What started out as a casual jog soon became a very serious pace.

As the summer progressed, Matt began to set goals for his running. One of these goals related back to that first run we had had together in the Canyon. Each year they hold a run in the Canyon, a half marathon. As Matt's running improved and the distances he covered grew, that race, the Spearfish Canyon half-marathon, became "our" dream. With that Spearfish race in the back of our minds we slowly but surely made our runs faster and longer. Our two-mile run became a three mile run, then a four-mile run and so on. I remember our first six-mile run was nothing more than a slow and steady shuffle. It took everything he had for Matt to make it back home that day. He was tired and exhausted, but would not quit at six miles. He was bound and determined to go farther. By the end of June, Matt had continued to progress and was becoming capable of beating me quite handily at the six-mile distance. We progressed up to a nine-mile run, then a ten-mile run, and then finally to a thirteen-mile run. Matt was now excited and feeling that the half-marathon was truly an attainable goal. He was determined to run the half marathon, and more than ever before, he was excited about the fall cross-country season at high school. Before too long he also had his mother, Janet, and friend, Josh talked into running the race, and plans to organize the trip began. As the date neared, with all of us firmly committed to the race, running was becoming a focal point of our entire family. We began to eat, drink and sleep determined to run the race. Matt began to push harder and harder, and by race day, was covering our regular six-mile loop under forty-minutes on a regular basis. I knew I was in trouble the night we ran the O'Gorman cross-country team's "Spencer Hill" workout. I made it up and down the hill five times, but could not keep up with Matt and had to "jog" home totally exhausted.

Daniel D. Deal

Matt ran up and down the hill ten times, and ran each loop one as fast as the one before it. To add insult to injury, he still caught me on the way home. I jogged into our driveway head down dripping with sweat, while he sprinted in bounding like a young hound dog. He was slowly becoming a real runner, and was developing the body and the drive to go with it. Because of this, I myself was developing into a proud papa and was enjoying every minute of it. After being a runner for over twenty-eight years, I was in shear heaven watching my son develop the same love for running I have always had.

CHAPTER 2
RACE DAY IN SPEARFISH

The weekend of the race was much like the first day Matt and I had ran together in Spearfish. It was again clear and sunny, though now a little warmer due to the mid-August season change. We arrived in Rapid City early on Friday and stopped at a truck stop for a pre-arranged meeting with Josh. Josh had been attending a church camp for the week, and was going to fit the half-marathon in between a prayer retreat and a rock climbing expedition. Once Josh joined us he and Matt chattered the entire way about their race strategies. This was the first race of this distance for both of them and they were very excited and anxious. Janet and I, on the other hand, were just hoping we could survive this day.

Race day arrived and the weather was gorgeous. The summer months had dried the Canyon out, and the trees and grass were a beautiful mixture of green, orange and brown. The heat and humidity were somewhat intense, but all in all it was going to be a wonderful day for running. We were careful to take plenty of fluids with us as we ventured to the park for the bus trip to the top of the hill. On the ride up I pointed out some of the other runners on the bus to Matt and Josh. We talked about some of the local running "celebrities," Fast Freddie, a masters runner who had been the Mayor of Spearfish and was still known for his ability to tear up race courses, with his speed. I pointed out some of the women runners who had won tons of races, and would probably be well in front of us today. I pointed out "Mountain Man Homer Hastings" a local legend who believes the only fair way to run the Spearfish race would be to make everyone turn around and run back up the hill at the end. This was one of those cult type races that was filled with many interesting people that gathered each year to run this race in one of the most beautiful places in the world.

The talk slowed as the bus reached the top of the canyon at Cheyenne Crossing. There the bus stopped. We unloaded and we jogged a half a mile or so down the hill. Josh and Matt were curious about where the rest rooms were so I pointed to the bushes along the road. Though reluctant at first, the boys did make a few trips into the bushes, before the race started. Finally, after months of preparation the gun sounded and we were all on our way in the Spearfish half-marathon. Josh took off immediately like a thoroughbred horse. He is a talented high school runner, who had been training throughout the summer with the goal of leading his cross-country team into the fall season. Matt and I were well aware of his ability so were a little more cautious, feeling our goal today should be to finish, and still be able to walk at the end of the day. We took the first mile slow, and looked back for Janet to see how she was coming. While we knew our day was going to be tiring, we also knew she had not trained as much for the race as she would have liked, and that it was going to be a long day for her. We were hoping optimistically she could finish, but knew that with the burden of caring for Andrew's broken leg she had not been able to get a lot of running in. She was probably going to struggle a lot today.

Matt, Josh and I began clicking the miles away rather comfortably. We used the first couple of miles to warm up then got into a nice pace for mile three, mile four, and mile five. We were cruising along at seven thirty to seven forty five per mile running pace. Josh was with us, just gliding along waiting for the right opportunity to sprint ahead and get down to some serious running. As we went along, we found small groups of people to run with, and tried to tag on with other runners keeping about the same pace. As we went around the curves of the canyon, we were often confronted with the motorcycles coming in huge packs directly at us. The annual Sturgis Motorcycle rally was scheduled to start the next day, and much of the crowd was already in the hills. The rally, which is now well into its sixtieth year, draws over a quarter of a million people some years, and packs the Black Hills with bikers from all over the world. Today, those bikers were somewhat of a nuisance as they were fighting for the same road we were running on. As we passed mile eight, we went around a curve and had to move over for several bikes. At mile nine, Josh's competitive juices were kicking in and he was ready to go. He was trying to bring Matt and I with him, but we were reluctant to go any faster. Josh really wanted to stay with Matt and make sure he was o.k., and asked several times how he was doing. Little did we know this was a theme and a line Josh would repeat several times during the next year? As Josh asked "Deal, how you doing?" Matt mumbled "o.k." At that point I encouraged Josh to go ahead, I would stay with Matt. After some hesitancy to leave his friend Josh took off. As we watched him leave, I don't think Matt or I had a clue how important Josh would become in our lives during the next few months. As we continued our run, Matt would surge some on the downhill, but strained as the course flattened out. I warned him that the last two miles were nearly flat, and that the running there would be more difficult. Now it was time to think about finishing. Mile eleven passed and Matt was struggling. Josh was now way ahead of us, but we could see him as he turned the corner and headed for the finish. He still looked as fresh as he had at the start of the race. True to my competitive spirit, each time I saw Josh I could feel my own pace picking up. I was trying to help Matt out as much as possible by taking the lead and letting him draft off of me, but at times it was obvious I was doing him more harm than good. This too would be a lesson for me to remember in the months ahead. I needed to push Matt, but I also needed to let him learn to handle what he could on his own. We continued to join groups of runners as we passed them, but the closer it came to the finish the less friendly people were becoming. Matt too, was now in that place where your body does only what your mind tells it to, and his mind was struggling to convince his body to keep moving. The look on his face was one of sheer determination. That is a face I now know all too well. My experience in having run over eighty marathons has taught me that at times like these it is sometimes best to be left alone to suffer. I left Matt just after mile eleven to let him deal with his inner demons alone. As I pulled away I didn't get much argument from him.

Graduating With Honor(s)

Josh finished the race in an all out sprint, whooping and hollering and passing runner after runner at the end. People were cheering and laughing at him as he was obviously having more fun than should be allowed at the finish of a long race. I pushed the pace as I neared the end of the race, but I was content with just rolling in so I could go back and help Matt. I finished and was very sore, but I was anxious to go back and see how Matt was doing as was Josh. When Josh and I got back to Matt he was about a quarter of a mile from the finish. Josh began running along beside Matt offering him encouragement and congratulating him on his run. Josh had a unique way of motivating Matt and keeping him on track. Matt seemed to respect Josh, and even more importantly he had utmost trust in Josh. As Matt neared the finish with Josh in tow he was struggling, but refusing to quit. He had come here to get this done, and he was now dug in and getting through it. Josh ran along side him offering all of the support and encouragement he could. Little did I realize, this would be just one of the many times that Josh would be encouraging Matt to continue on while he was struggling in pain. Matt's final time for the half marathon was in the mid- one forties. It was a respectable time, and I think better than he had really anticipated. Once he crossed the finish line the pain and agony immediately turned to a sense of joy. He had done what he had come here to do, and he was now feeling very proud. He had accomplished one of the first big goals he had set for himself this year, and he had done it well. We now waited for Janet to struggle in and to our surprise she came in slowly but comfortably staying well within herself the entire race. When it was all said and done she probably had run the smartest race, staying nice and comfortable not hurting herself and enjoying the scenery along the course as she went. She was joined in the last miles by Chris, Andrew, and their cousins Sam and Logan. While they were sure they were helping, the look on Janet's face was more one of "who the heck are these jokers?" After a few post race pictures and a change of clothes we were quickly off to get Josh rock climbing. Josh followed the half marathon by joining his church group for an afternoon of prayer and rock climbing. Matt and I returned to Spearfish for an afternoon of rest and relaxation.

CHAPTER 3
OUR SENIOR YEAR

The next few weeks went extremely quickly. The week after we returned from Spearfish, Matt began getting up early to run with his high school cross-country team. He would then go to marching band practice. Like most seniors, he was excited about his senior year, and was feeling good about the months ahead. Matt was pumped early on about running, saying he was feeling good and strong. He knew he would need to work on his speed, but he felt confident he could run all day long if he needed to. He had always enjoyed band having made most of his high school friendships there. He had met Josh in band and his other best friend Jason. Matt and Jason called themselves "Dumb and Dumber" and when the three of them were together they referred to themselves as "Dumb and Dumber and Runner." Jason is known to have a very creative sense of humor. Jason's sense of humor was something that Matt would need in the months ahead. Jason, like Josh could get through to Matt like nobody else could, and like Josh Jason was to become a very important part of Matt's life in the months ahead.

During the next few weeks Matt got up early each morning and came home whistling and singing at the end of the school day. He was no doubt enjoying his senior year. This was supposed to be the time of his life. Matt was obviously having fun and looking forward to the year ahead. His goals for the year were to make the varsity cross-country team, graduate with honors and get a 4.0 grade point average. While Matt was working hard and was very excited about all of the things that were going on in his life, I was lamenting the loss of my summer friend and running partner. I knew his senior year was supposed to be one of gradual separation from the family, as he gained his independence and ventured off to college. But I didn't know it would start this soon. While I still ran during my noon hours with a group of friends, the time I had spent this summer with Matt was being deeply missed.

School started for Matt with a tremendous high. Like most seniors he was on top of the world and feeling it. He was running well, enjoying band, and taking some very difficult classes. Matt loved the challenge of academics and had always pushed himself to get good grades and to be one of the top students in his class. Matt had always been a 4.0 student and planned to finish his senior year with a bang. He wanted to work toward some college scholarships, visit some colleges down south, and spend his senior year as a stepping stone to college and a career.

Once school started it was just a matter of a few weeks before Matt's mood went from one of excitement to one of frustration. His workouts quickly became work, his energy level began to wane, and it was starting to be a struggle for him to just drag himself out of bed in the morning. What had been easy jogs for him this summer were now becoming very difficult runs. While he had always been dedicated to the early morning marching band practices, he was now unable to get himself out of bed, and began having a difficult time just making it through the school day.

As he continued to struggle, we tried to convince him that possibly all he needed was rest, but he argued it was more than just being tired. After watching Matt compete in a couple of races where he seemed to struggle just to survive, I began to question whether or not he was trying hard enough, and if he was really working as hard as he thought. These were questions I will regret thinking for the rest of my life. Matt continued running and marching in band and became more committed then ever to push himself through the tiredness and pain he was beginning to have. We continued to tell him it was stress, and that being tired at his age was normal. Matt seemed to be getting upset because we did not understand how tired and achy he was really feeling. We have second-guessed ourselves a million times about what we should have done during this time.

As we continued to encourage Matt by telling him he was just stressed and tired, he seemed to push even harder. I knew he could run faster. We had run workouts this summer faster than he was now running races. We talked about stress and the need to rest more. Matt reluctantly listened, but the doubt in his eyes was obvious, he knew more was going on than just fatigue and stress.

The next race, Matt set his goal to win the Junior Varsity race. When the race began he seemed comfortable and looked like his old self. As the race progressed Matt began to struggle more and more until he finally fell way off the pace and finished well behind the top runners.

Though he had finished well enough to win a place medal, Matt was discouraged both at how he had run, and at how much effort the race had taken. He said he just did not understand why he felt so bad. He said it actually hurt to run, and he was feeling horrible. The previous summer he and I had run faster than he had today and he never once felt that poorly. After that race he began complaining that something was seriously wrong and that he just was not feeling right. He said he needed to rest, and knew he needed something more than just some time off. When Matt arrived home that day he went right to bed and slept the rest of the weekend. We could begin to see the change in his eyes. He no longer had that bright optimistic look about him. He was beginning to look tired and scared. We knew he was tired and run down, however we knew something was seriously wrong when that weekend he did not even bother doing his homework. It was the first time in his entire high school career that he had not done his homework. Matt lived for his grades, and when he went to school on Monday without it done, we knew something was seriously wrong.

As the next week began, Matt's condition worsened to the point that he could not get up to participate in either band or cross-country. He had a history of sinus problems, so we took him to the doctor and they put him on antibiotics. Matt took the next couple of days off from school, and though he still did not feel better, he tried to return to both band and running on Wednesday. A couple of more days passed, but by the weekend he was not feeling any better. The cross-country team had a big trip planned to Minneapolis and since Matt was not scheduled to

Graduating With Honor(s)

run we let him go along despite not feeling well. He promised he would rest, and we made Josh and Jason promise to make sure he didn't do too much. When he returned from the trip he was better but still not himself. He struggled through a couple more days of school then realizing he was not improving we made another trip to the doctor. This time the doctor diagnosed Matt with mono. The treatment was bed rest, and plenty of fluids. Though he had been feeling poorly, Matt had continued trying to do too much. The doctor's orders were now clear; rest, rest, and more rest. It was now confirmed that Matt was legitimately sick. He now would need to take even more care to rest and get plenty of fluids. We were all hoping with a little rest, a little luck, and a little prayer; that Matt would soon be back on his feet and up to full speed. Little did we know at this point what we would be up against for the remainder of the year.

CHAPTER 4
REST, REST AND MORE REST

The next four weeks Matt did absolutely nothing. He spent twenty fours hours a day locked up in his basement bedroom. During this time he slept constantly and could muster barely enough energy to climb the basement stairs for a drink of water. We insisted that he drink plenty of fluids and started giving him handfuls of vitamins every day. Though Matt had always been an honor student and was a member of the National Honor Society as a junior, he was making only a feeble attempt to keep up with his schoolwork, and was beginning to go days without even looking at his books. By now Janet and I were growing more and more concerned with each passing day. As a nurse Janet was well aware of the toll mono could have, but even in the most severe cases it did not seem like they hung on this long. Matt was slowly going from tired to run down, to simply not seeming to care. Matt had always been driven when it came to studying, and his lack of interest in schoolwork should have told us something was seriously wrong. As he began to fall further and further behind in his schoolwork there was a growing concern about whether or not he would be able to catch up. Matt called Josh and Jason and had them bring his assignments and notes over for him to read. Matt gave the homework a cursory once over, but really was not getting much done. He called Josh and had him come over on a couple of occasions to help him with Calculus assignments, but for the most part Matt just did not have the energy to even act interested. One night he and I went over some notes of Jason's but when we realized neither of us could read them we gave up in a well needed laugh. We decided we didn't know if we were working harder to learn the material or to learn Jason's hand writing. We had a great time trying to decipher Jason's scribbles.

As the days grew into weeks, and Matt missed more and more school, Jason and Jason's girlfriend Emily came over more and more often trying to cheer Matt up. Matt was just too tired to do much visiting and was growing more and more listless as the weeks passed. As the weekends came and went we kept wishing we could get Matt to school events or out of the house, but knew, at that same time, that he needed his rest. He was in a downward spiral that was really beginning to concern us. Matt continued to grow more and more pale, and was losing weight. He continued complaining about a tingling and soreness in his legs, but could not really come up with any real clear symptoms that pointed to anything being wrong other than a severe case of mono.

As we entered into the fifth week of his illness Matt began to feel a little better and we began making plans for him to return to school for a least half days during the second week of October. We had planned a trip to Minneapolis to watch a Minnesota Vikings and Green Bay Packers Football Game, but were not sure Matt was strong enough to make the trip. When the day of the game came, Matt said he felt better and was willing to give it a try. He knew this trip meant the world to his little brother Andrew who is a fanatic Packers fan, and there was no way Matt was going to spoil this for Andrew's sake, no matter how sick he was. Though he looked like death warmed over when he woke up that morning we headed out early for the four-hour trip to the Metrodome in the Twin Cities.

Matt slept most of the way to the game, but he seemed to be have a pretty good time during the game itself though as the game progressed Matt talked less and less. Even Brett Farve throwing a touch down did not get him going. Toward the end of the game it was obvious he was tired, but he continued to work at hanging in there. As we left the stadium we had a three or four block walk back to our vehicle and the parking ramp. As we neared the ramp Matt slowed considerably and began complaining that his legs hurt. As we got to the ramp he asked me to bring the van down to him to pick him up. He said his legs hurt and he did not think he could make it to the van. He continued to struggle on, but by the time we reached the van Matt was clinging to doors and to walls to hold him self up. He crawled into the van and complained that his legs were burning and hurting. Matt made it to the back of the van and strapped himself in. He fell asleep almost right away and slept the entire four-hour ride home. When we got home that night he went right to bed and slept the entire night. We wrote it off to his first big day out, and were still hoping he was on the road to recovery.

CHAPTER 5
IT NOW GETS REAL

The next morning Matt got up and went to school as planned. He was excited to get back into a normal routine. He got up showered and was off to school at the normal time and place. For the first time in a couple of months, we all breathed a sigh of relief, because we were back to normal. We all had our fingers crossed that the mono was now behind Matt and that he would be able to get back to being himself.

The excitement of the day lasted until about 5:00 p.m. When I returned home from work, Matt was on the upstairs couch exhausted. He had come home from school and fallen asleep right away. When he woke up he began complaining that his legs hurt and were tingling. We thought that he was just overtired from his first day back at school and encouraged him to rest. He was planning to attend the cross-country banquet that evening, and we were excited to go. Though he had missed almost the entire season, tonight would be the first time in quite a while that we would actually be part of a school activity. As the time for the banquet neared we told Matt he should get up to get ready. He was unable to move because he was tired, and he complained that his legs were hurting him. We got his clothes etc, and pleaded with him to go. It would be good for him; he had been in bed for weeks, and we were worried he was getting depressed and not trying hard enough. But as the time neared, Matt just could not go… He ended up sleeping most of the evening, and woke up only to watch a little television and eat.

Around 10:00 that evening the doorbell rang. It was Lynn, Ann and Josh Tschetter. This was the first time of many that God would send these angels to us. While Matt had been a friend with Josh for some time, we had not been real close friends with the Tschetters. During Matt's bout with mono they had called a few times, and Josh had brought over Matt's school assignments and tried to help him with some homework, sometimes late into the night. Tonight they had come over with pictures from the cross-country season that had been handed out at the banquet this evening. Lynn and Ann were very concerned about Matt, and said they knew he was still ill due to the fact that he did not even make it to the banquet. They also said Josh had wanted to make sure "Deal" was o.k., so he wanted to stop on the way home to see Matt. From this point on, it seemed like Josh, Lynn and Ann were always there at the times when it was the most difficult for Matt. Josh was to prove to be a true friend, and though Janet and I hardly knew the Tschetter family at this point, they would become a very important part of our lives in the weeks and months ahead. Were it not for Josh, Jason, and Matt's other friends, I really do not know how we would have even faced the months ahead. That night the Tschetters had brought over an award which was to have been presented to Matt at the cross-country awards banquet. He had won an award for running the most miles last summer. The award was called The "Riggen" award. In presenting it, the coach apparently spoke about how Matt had not given up this year despite all of the obstacles he had faced. He had been an inspiration to the team because of the way he had tried to fight through his illness. We were horribly disappointed that we were not at the banquet, and felt bad that Matt was not able to be there when he was recognized for all of his hard work. Little did we know how much hard work Matt had ahead of him! That night, the Tschetter's convinced Janet and I to take Matt to the emergency room. The ER staff could not find anything further wrong with him, but felt he might be dehydrated. They gave Matt a liter of fluids, and sent him home to rest, hoping the fluids would begin to perk him up.

The next morning Matt was not feeling well at all and was not able to make it up for school. He complained that he was weak and his legs were feeling "tingly." I remember Janet feeling bad about calling in sick for him. He had missed six weeks of school and now was supposed to be recuperated. We were beginning to wonder just how long this was going to go on. The joke in the house was that after hearing our voices every day the attendance staff was surely getting tired of it. There was a television commercial for comedian Ray Stevens. He had a song that went "Yea, its me again Margaret." Margaret was the attendance person's name. The joke around the house when we had to call in for Matt was "Yea its me again Margaret". It seemed like Matt had been sick for a lifetime, and it did not look like he was going to be getting well any time soon.

As a nurse Janet was usually the one that ended up dealing with most of Matt's medical complaints. When he did not feel well again the next morning she called our family doctor and took Matt in for more tests. Matt was more than willing to go to the doctor and did so without complaint. This was our first clue that Matt was sick, and that he was also beginning to worry about what was going on. He had always complained about going to the doctor, but now he was more than willing to go without protest.

After calling our family doctor he recommended we go to the hospital for further evaluation. That afternoon he had us consult with a neurologist and they began running some tests. When we got home from the hospital late that night, it was well after midnight. We were beginning to realize there was something seriously wrong with Matt. As would be the case in the months ahead, there were messages on our answering machine that night from the Tschetters, and from Jason. Matt had no idea how lucky he was to have made friends like these.

The neurologist ran several tests on Matt but could not find anything wrong. The emergency room doctor believed Matt was suffering from dehydration so they gave him more fluids. This was starting to become regular protocol for Matt, and each time they gave him fluids he looked at us like they were crazy. The doctors advised us to begin pushing fluids with Matt at home and once again sent us on our way.

The next day was another call to Margaret in the school attendance office. We were now becoming seriously concerned about Matt's grades. He had missed all of the marching band season, and was now falling seriously behind in school. Matt had always been an "A" student, but now he had absolutely no interest in school or his grades. This was not the senior year we had hoped for. Matt was beginning to fall way behind, and was missing most everything associated with his senior year.

Matt spent most of the next day on the couch, and began complaining more and more about the tingling and pain in his legs. He complained that it hurt for him to even walk to the bathroom. He continued to eat very little and we were beginning to grow increasingly concerned that something was seriously wrong. Matt just did not have any energy, was hurting all over, and just did not seem to have any motivation to fight back. He had been sick for nearly two months at this point, and the mental wear and tear was beginning to show. He eyes were black and sunken and his skin was growing a pale yellow. Janet was growing very impatient and wanted some answers. She scheduled another appointment with the doctor. They ran some more tests on Matt but again could not find anything. They again sent him home, but this time when we got home he could not even walk in the door. He complained that his legs were weak, and that they hurt. Janet and I had to carry him in and lay him on the couch because by now he was complaining that the pain was excruciating. The worry was beginning to show on our faces, and both Chris and Andrew began asking what was wrong. They were becoming very frightened for their older brother. It was quickly becoming apparent that Matt was now suffering from more than just mono.

Matt was feeling even worse the next morning so we made another trip to the hospital. The seriousness of what we were dealing with was now beginning to become more apparent. The doctors scheduled a MRI, a spinal tap and several neurological tests. They were attempting to rule out several things with Matt including MS and Meningitis. Matt was to have the MRI done the first thing that morning. He would then have a spinal tap done, after which he would be required to lay in recovery for a couple of hours until the injection site had healed. Janet pushed for them to do the spinal tap first, then have Matt do the MRI since he would need to lie flat anyway. The nurses were reluctant to change the orders, but for the first time during this whole ordeal, I saw the "nurse" in Janet come out and she began to take charge of Matt's care. Her patience had worn thin with weeks of not getting answers and the mom/nurse in her kicked in. This is the first time I remember us taking control of Matt's treatment, but it would not be the last. As we would find in the weeks and months ahead, if we did not demand or insist on things they just did not get done. We were lucky Janet had the medical knowledge she had, because it made a very difficult journey a little easier. She insisted that day that the doctors do the spinal tap first and then the MRI. Matt had been sick so long, and had suffered so much, that she just was not willing to watch him suffer needlessly.

Once we got down to the testing area we waited a brief time, then they took us to the room for the spinal tap. Once the spinal tap was complete they took Matt down for the MRI. He would need to lie still in a huge machine for two or three hours while they took images of his entire body. Matt had brought a music tape along that he wanted to listen to, and for the first time this morning actually acted like a teenager again. He wanted specific tapes and specific music to listen to. He complained that the songs we had were not the right ones, and that this whole thing was a waste of time. Janet and I smiled at each other, this was the first time we had seen Matt fight back in some time, and we were happy, in a weird sort of way, to hear him arguing. This was the first spark we had seen in him since he first contracted mono. That was a spark Matt needed to keep alive so he could face the long winding road ahead. We had arrived at the hospital shortly before 8:00 that morning and they completed the final tests around 3:00. Once they were done with all of the tests they took Matt back to the recovery room while we waited for the results. Matt continued to rest for a few more hours and by now we had been in the hospital for nearly nine hours. The nurse came in and said if Matt was doing o.k. he could go home and they would call us with the results. His pain was growing steadily worse, and he was now at the point where he was not even able to walk. He said his legs were weak and hurt too much to stand on them. We had no idea how we were going to get him home.

The nurse saw our predicament, and offered a hospital wheel chair to get Matt to our van and into our house. The problem was that once we got home, Janet and I would have to carry Matt into our house and down a flight of stairs. We wheeled Matt from the recovery room to the van, then lifted him carefully into the back seat. He screamed in pain when we touched him, and he was unable to find a position on the seat that did not hurt. By now he was clenching his teeth and wincing constantly due to the pain. Whatever this was it seemed to be progressing rapidly. At this point Janet and I were trying our best not to panic. We had no idea what do to do, and I was becoming increasingly upset that they had even sent Matt home in that condition. When we got home to our driveway Matt's pain had progressed to the point that I knew there was no way we could take him into the house. I told Janet she needed to go into the house, call the doctor and tell him what was going on. I did not want Matt to know how panicked we were, but the pain he was experiencing was obviously the sign of something very wrong. Janet told the doctor that Matt's pain was growing worse by the minute, and that he was complaining about tingling and numbness in his feet. The doctor was in the process of reading the tests, and decided that based on the results of the MRI, blood work and his symptoms, maybe it was best if they did admit Matt overnight to see how things progressed. We hurried back to the hospital as quickly as we could, with Matt screaming in pain in the back seat.

When we got back to the hospital they admitted Matt immediately, taking him right from our van to a room transferring him via a wheel chair. By now he was obviously scared to death and in agonizing pain. They admitted Matt to a floor on neurology, and began administering I.V. fluids and mild pain medications to take the edge off the pain and discomfort he was feeling. As the night progressed, Matt's pain continued to grow worse. It was becoming obvious that whatever it was it was continuing to progress and that his symptoms were beginning to worsen. From 9:00 that morning until 9:00 that evening his pain had intensified one hundred times over. The doctor continued to increase the amount of pain medications and gave Matt something to sleep, so he finally settled down a bit.

Since Chris and Andrew had been alone during this time I went home to get them to bed while Janet stayed with Matt at the hospital sleeping on a couch at the foot of his bed. While it made more sense for me to go home, I don't think an army could have drug Janet away from Matt's bedside at that point. The stress she would have on her for the next several months was just beginning, and the weariness was already showing on her face.

On the way home I cried for the first time during the incident. I knew something very serious was wrong, but I did not know what. I just had a sense by looking at Matt, and seeing the fear in his eyes, that he was worried he was going to die. Though unsaid, I think all of us were having the same thoughts. I had never seen anyone in that much pain. All I could remember was when my father had had his leg amputated as a result of his diabetes. Even after that surgery, they were able to control the pain quite easily with drugs. It seemed like Matt's pain was not responding to the pain medications, and through the course of the evening they needed to give him more and more drugs to keep the pain under control. He was a strong young man, but whatever this was he was fighting was taking all of his strength.

When I got to the hospital the next day they were running more tests. Matt's condition had continued to worsen, and the pain and numbness in his feet and legs was now unbearable. The doctors knew by now that there was something neurological going on, but they did not know what. The doctor we had was new to the area, and had just come from the Mayo Clinic. He was known to be very thorough and very knowledgeable in neurology. The nurses said he was the best doctor in town to be treating this kind of an illness, and he was running every test imaginable trying to find out what was going on. With Janet's nursing background she had good understanding of the various tests and laboratory results that were ordered for Matt. If she did not understand something she called the doctors she worked for and had them explain it to her. She also called her brother-in-law Bob in Spearfish whenever she had any questions. Bob was more or less our final authority on things, as we trusted his judgement immensely. We were making sure we were doing everything possible. Even at that, it was not enough.

As the day progressed, they began ruling out things like spinal meningitis, viruses, and rare diseases such as Guillain Barre Syndrome. The good news was that each of the tests was coming up negative; the bad news was that Matt's pain and symptoms were growing worse by the hour. By late afternoon he was describing his pain as a seven on a scale of one to ten. A scale he and the rest of us would get to know real well during the months ahead. As the day progressed into evening, the pain began to move toward an eight, then a nine. The pain medications they were giving Matt continued to grow stronger, but their ability to keep him comfortable was becoming marginal at best. As we moved into the late evening, Janet and I could no longer tolerate watching

Matt struggle in pain. He was crying, beginning to have seizure like shakes, and was scared to death. He could no longer feel his toes or feet, and was beginning to complain that he could not feel his fingers or hands anymore. It was Friday evening, and it was obvious we were going to be in for a long night. There had been no school that day, and many students and faculty from Matt's school began calling. They had heard that Matt had been hospitalized and the concern and prayers began immediately. These calls would be the first of thousands that we would receive during the next days and weeks. It was these calls and the unbelievable support we received from the "O'Gorman" family that would literally carry us through this whole ordeal.

As Matt's pain continued that night, Janet and I could no longer watch Matt struggle in such agony, and we insisted the nurses contact the doctor for some additional pain medication. They were reluctant to call the doctor at home, but as Matt's fear and pain grew worse. A male nurse on the unit began to take charge. He began comforting Matt and made the calls to help us get the medication to ease Matt's pain. The doctor was reluctant to give too much medication concerned that the drugs might mask the symptoms Matt was experiencing. Matt now was describing his pain as a ten out of ten on the pain scale, and told one nurse the only pain he could imagine that would be worse than this was being shot and laying in a pool of blood bleeding to death. We were adamant. Give him all of the pain medication he needed. We could no longer stand by and watch him struggle in so much pain.

Janet sat with Matt that whole night holding him, massaging him and trying to ease his pain with cool towels and soothing words. While I was reluctant to leave, one of us had to go home to be with the other boys. In the middle of all of this, we had to try to keep some normalcy in our lives. Janet and I made the commitment right away that we would expose Chris and Andrew to as little of Matt's suffering as managable, and work to keep their lives as normal as possible. We knew already that this would probably have a great impact on family, and the more we could keep things as routine as possible the better. I think we sensed already at this point that our lives were going to be changing in one way or another from what was going on with Matt. This had already gone on for over seven weeks, and for now it did not appear that this ordeal would be ending soon. The shots they were now giving him were holding the pain off for an hour maybe two, but then Matt would wake up screaming, now in even more pain than before. By morning the pain had grown to the point that the shots were almost completely ineffective. When I returned to the hospital the next day I was not prepared for what I would see. Matt was soaking wet. He was drenched in sweat from the pain. His legs were shaking, his body was in spasms and he was conscious only long enough to request more pain medication. He now screamed at even the touch of the bed sheets to his body. He was scared to death. He looked at us with the look only a parent who has had a seriously ill child would understand. That look, like "Mom, Dad, what is happening to me"?

When the doctor came in the next day he spent hours pouring through the charts and reviewing the tests. He examined Matt, and reported to us that his neurological symptoms were growing worse, but they still really did not know what he had, or what was going on. We pushed for more pain medication for Matt, but he said that would only mask the symptoms. The doctor said he would stop back later that day to check Matt again, but at this point he really did not have any answers. Matt's pain was now clearly out of control. He was lying in pools of water from the sweat and he was shaking and screaming from the pain. He would moan "help me, help me, oh, oh, someone help me!" The nurses were making him get up to go to the bathroom, and it was becoming obvious he could no longer walk on his feet, or bear his own weight. Each time he took a step he said it was like walking on hot coals. He was scared to death, as were we. We had no idea what was happening to him.

CHAPTER 6
A NIGHT IN HELL, A VISIT FROM HEAVEN

When the doctor came back that evening he still had no answers. We were very frustrated by now, explaining Matt could no longer deal with the pain, and that he was scared to death. The doctor told us we needed to stay calm, and we need to reassure Matt that everything would be o.k. He told us that for Matt to stay strong we needed to stay strong. Matt just could not see us break down. He also said that the use of drugs would reduce Matt's ability to deal with the pain in the long term, and that we needed to continue pushing Matt to get up to deal with pain. The doctor said the more Matt let the pain win, the longer his recovery would take. He did not know for sure what was going on. He thought it was possibly a version of Guillain Barre, but said Matt's blood work lacked the protein and other characteristics needed to make the diagnosis. They were also surprised that Matt was not losing muscle strength, so they wanted to continue to watch him before they became too aggressive in their treatment. This was not something they had seen before, so they did not want to act too hastily. The doctor left late that Saturday afternoon providing us few answers. I remember Janet beginning to cry. I was in a daze. I got up and walked down the hallway and totally lost it. I remember feeling totally helpless.

In the meantime, we heard the call we have heard a million times since, "Mom, Dad"? It was Matt; he was scared to death and wanting us. From that point on he just never really seemed to want to be alone. He has always wanted one of us near him. We began doing that day what we have done a thousand times since. We each took a deep breath, gathered our strength and went to his bedside to be with him. I cannot count the times since this first happened that he has called out to us, and we have had to compose ourselves to go to his side.

When we got in Matt's room he cried because he could no longer feel his fingers and hands. His legs were shaking and he began clinching his arms to his chest in a spastic sort of way. His toes began curling into the bottoms of his feet to the point that his toenails were actually cutting the bottoms of his feet. He began grinding his teeth, and was literally pouring sweat from the pain. Janet and I watched this for another couple of hours in sheer terror. I became angry, she became a nurse, assessing, reassessing, and trying to communicate with Matt. We were continually asking the nurses for answers, but they had very few to offer us. It was obvious they had no answers for Matt's pain, or our questions. The plan was to wait and see. They were unable to do little for Matt and his screaming and shaking were more than Janet and I were able to handle.

This continued until about nine-o clock that evening. By then Janet, Matt and I had about all we could take. His pain and symptoms continued to worsen, and the shots for pain the nurses were giving him now did absolutely nothing. Matt again had the male nurse who we now learned was named Chris. We shared our concerns with Chris and said we wanted to talk to the doctor and that we felt this just could not go on. Chris checked into it for us and found our doctor was not on call and that he was gone for the weekend. Janet knew the doctor on call, but she did not feel someone unfamiliar with the case could just walk in and change what our doctor was doing. As Matt began to suffer more and more, and the shots were no longer even mildly effective, Janet made a decision that would be one of many decisions we ourselves would need to make. If Matt was going to get through this, and get better, we might have to be more aggressive and take things into our own hands. The doctors and nurses were obviously very busy, and simply hoping they were able to keep up with Matt's care just might not be enough. I think that evening, we realized <u>WE</u> were going to have to be responsible for Matt's care. If he was going to get better, we were going to have to find out what was going on, and be aggressive in treating it. There are no case managers or care teams, if Matt was to improve, <u>WE</u> would need to coordinate the care. Unfortunately that burden began to fall on Janet right away. She quickly became responsible for directing Matt's care. She had to ask the right questions, make the decisions, and then hope we were doing the right thing. From that very first night, it became clear, we were dealing with something that was quite different than the doctors and hospital staff had dealt with before, and we were going to need to figure much of this out for ourselves. At 9:30 pm on that Saturday night Janet began taking things into her own hands. Her first decision was that Matt could not struggle through this pain all weekend. At times, he looked like he was going to pass out due to the constant pain, and that was with his shots of pain medication! Janet began telling the nurses that Matt needed something more for pain, but there was nothing else in the orders. Janet asked if they could call the doctor on call, but the physician on call was unwilling to interfere with our doctors orders and protocol for care.

At around 10:30 p.m. Janet simply could not sit by without doing anything. She called a local neurologist she knew, at home, and began telling her about Matt and what we wanted done. Dr. Miles was a neurologist in town who Janet had seen for migraines. Janet was very comfortable with her, and made the decision, at that point, that she wanted Dr. Miles to be Matt's doctor. Part of this decision was the fact that we needed and wanted Matt to get some relief now, and part of it was the fact that Janet knew Dr. Miles, and felt comfortable telling her what we were wanting. Janet talked with Matt's nurse about it and though he assured us the doctor we had was the very best, Janet still felt strongly that she wanted Dr. Miles to take over the case. While they still did not seem to know what they were dealing with, we knew emotionally this was going to be difficult on us, and we needed to be able to feel comfortable with the doctor at all levels.

When Janet called Dr. Miles, she was at a cook out with other doctors from her practice. Ironically, the on-call doctor was at her house, and she was already aware that we had called him and that he was unwilling to interfere with the other doctors orders. Dr. Miles visited with Janet for some time and consulted with the on call doctor. She knew Janet was a nurse, and she knew Janet as a patient. Dr. Miles was also aware that Janet is quite level headed and is a very capable nurse. She had to assume that if things were to such a point that Janet was calling her at home, and feeling things were this far out of control, that Matt was probably getting worse. Janet talked with Dr. Miles for some time, and told her we wanted Matt's pain under control, and that we wanted his care to be more aggressive. We were very concerned with the pain levels that Matt was having and that even if he physically recovered, emotionally he would be a wreck from what he was going through. As the director of a counseling agency that deals with victims of Post Traumatic Stress Syndrome, I could not imagine that Matt would not suffer long term trauma from what he was going through. He was dealing with constant pain that he identified as a ten out of ten on the pain scale, and at times, he appeared nearly incoherent as he screamed and shook. Janet told Dr. Miles during their conversation that we wanted her as Matt's doctor, and that we needed relief for Matt right now. Since we did not know what direction this whole thing was going, we at least wanted Matt to be peaceful if things got worse. We wanted pain medications; serious pain medications, and for the hospital staff to quit getting Matt out of bed. We wanted Matt to get some relief. His pain was unbearable, and at this point letting it go did not seem to be helping anything. We did not know what Matt had. If this did continue and he did get worse, Janet and I could not live with ourselves knowing we were let him suffer like that.

Janet told Dr. Miles we did not really know the other physician, but at this point we wanted some things to happen right now, and we

Graduating With Honor(s)

were calling on her to help us. Dr. Miles consulted with the on-call Dr. and agreed to begin trying some more aggressive pain medications. They began a morphine pump, gave Matt some Valium, and shots of Viscaril. They talked about a drug called Neurotin for the nerves, and the possibility of having a psychiatric consult done in the morning. Janet also asked that Dr. Miles explain to our other doctor that we made decisions without him because we needed something done, and done right away. We did not feel we could wait any longer. We were unwilling to let Matt suffer for one minute longer than he needed to. Dr. Miles agreed to come up and see Matt the next day, Sunday. When Janet hung up that evening she could not believe what she had done. She did not know if we had made the right decision or not. She could not believe she had called Dr. Miles at home, on a Saturday night, but we knew from this point on that if Matt was going to get better, we were going to have to make many hard, hard decisions.

The next hour passed rather slowly, the pain medications still did not help, and the nurse said it might take a while for them to catch up with the pain before Matt would begin to feel more comfortable. By now, I was crying constantly and could not stand to be in the room watching Matt suffer. He was seizing in pain, and was soaking his bed from sweating so much from the pain. He was now complaining that even the hospital gown hurt to touch his skin. He had no socks on, no sheets on the bed, and he had his feet propped on pillows. He complained that even touching his heels to the pillows was like knives cutting his flesh. His nurse was now spending nearly all of his time in the room comforting Matt, talking with us, and working diligently to get the meds on board as quickly as possible. I think, he too, realized the pain was out of control, and that things were getting to a critical point. The scene continued to get worse, and the panic was beginning to set in for all of us. We kept asking Matt what we could do. We offered water, soda, wet towels, etc, but nothing eased his pain or calmed the panic he was feeling. He began to cry, and he could not control his arms or legs any longer. They were in constant spasms, and Matt was panicked about what was happening. He began to cry and said he did not know why God and everyone else had given up on him. He did not know why he was being punished and why this was happening to him. Finally, around 11:00 p.m. that Saturday night, feeling he was at the end of his rope, Matt asked us to call "Josh."

Janet and I just looked at each other, and wondered how we could bring a young person in to see this. How would Josh respond? Would he freak out? Would he run from the room in tears? We just did not know how you call a high school student at 11:00 at night and ask them to do what we needed. But at this point we were desperate.

Josh had moved to O'Gorman in the ninth grade, and he and Matt had become friends though cross-country and band. They had gone on band and cross-country trips together, and Matt had gone on a couple of church retreats with Josh during the past few summers. This was the same Josh who had run the Spearfish ½ marathon with us last summer, and he had been over to the house several times while Matt was sick with mono. I remember one evening when Matt was struggling with his

Calculus class. Josh had run that evening, gone to a school function, then at 9:30 at night came over to help Matt get caught up with his assignments. I remember watching them in the living room I did not know who was more tired, Josh or Matt. They worked until nearly 11 o'clock that night, and I remember thinking, I wish I had had friends like that growing up. Little did I know that night, what kind of a friend Josh *really* was! Janet and I were beside ourselves and did not know what to do. Finally around 11:00 that night, we realized we had to call Josh.

Janet reached Josh's mom Ann just before 11:00 that night. They had just gotten home from a trip to Minneapolis where they had gone to the Mall of America. We did not know how to ask, or what to ask, but explained to them that Matt was in the hospital and not doing well. The one thing he wanted was to see Josh. While we knew it was a lot to ask, we were desperate, and asked if Josh could possibly come to the hospital to see Matt now. At 11:00 on a Saturday night, we were calling people we hardly knew reaching out in desperation. We were scared to death, and at this point, were even having thoughts of whether Matt would live or die.

The Tschetters arrived at the hospital late that night looking tired and road weary. They had obviously had a long day of their own, and we were about to make it longer for them. As Josh peaked into the room I wanted to warn him about what he would see, Matt was shaking, nearly convulsing in pain, his bed was soaked from the sweat, and his arms, face and legs were contorted from the pain. He had thrown off all of the sheets and blankets because it hurt to have them touch his skin. Matt laid in a soaked hospital gown, screaming in agony. Before I could warn Josh about what he would see, he was already in the room and without hesitation went to Matt's bedside and began holding him. His quiet "Hey Deal" was all Matt needed. Though Matt still struggled, he became much stronger and more at peace once Josh entered the room. When I later asked Matt why it was Josh he wanted to see that night he responded. **"Because I knew he could handle it".**

Josh sat and held Matt that night. He took Matt's hands and kept them from shaking. He continued to tell Matt he would be fine, and that he was o.k. I don't know if it was Josh, the drugs, or a combination of the two, but by 1:30 or 2:00 that morning Matt had begun to calm down completely. The shaking was considerably better, the pain was more tolerable, and Matt was able to drift off into a deep sleep. Matt continued to hit the button on the morphine pump every ten to fifteen minutes, struggling to keep the pain at bay. The nurses later told us the button had been pushed thirty times during the night.

While Josh sat with Matt, his parents Lynn and Ann talked with Janet and I. They sat with us early into the morning hugging and praying. Once Matt fell into a deep morphine sleep, Josh emerged from the room. He looked tired and emotionally drained. Ann hugged him several times, then the five of us joined hands in a circle of prayer. A prayer for healing, for guidance, and for patience. Ann said it that night and many times since. *"God works in mysterious ways, and in his own way and time. He had given Matt this burden to bear for a reason, a reason none of us would understand. But this was something that was in God's plan for Matt and for those of us around Matt. Like many things God does, none of us will ever really understand why this happened to Matt."*

But it became clear very early on, that Matt and a lot of other people would grow tremendously through this ordeal. It was no doubt a way to bring a family, a school, and in some respects a community, closer together. God had a plan for Matt and all of us that night and every night since Matt was stricken with this horrible disease. We just had to be patient and let God's plan for Matt unfold as it surely would.

When the Tschetters left that night a calm had fell over us. We were completely exhausted but filled with adrenaline. Their words and prayers had been very uplifting and encouraging. Though everything seemed very dark and lonely that night, something about their visit had given us the sense that it would be all right. They had given us the strength to realize that this was not in our hands, it was in God's hands. There was a higher power in control, and the Tschetters had reminded us of that fact. Josh and their entire family had been strong enough to let us see, we were not in charge, and that we had to let the true God who was in charge work His will. This was an important lesson for us at an important time. For now, we had the strength to go on.

While Matt was in his room pumping morphine to ease the pain, Janet and I had a chance to relax and seek some relief from the pain ourselves. Janet went and sat at Matt's bedside, while I walked down the hall and tried to make some sense of what was happening. What was happening to the world we knew? The safe world we had come to know, working and running and being a family? As I walked, I breathed a deep sigh of relief. I knew that despite everything we needed to be strong and to have the courage to help Matt. We also had to be strong for Chris and Andrew. This would be devastating for them. I knew that for now we needed to concentrate, and to let our friends step in when the burden became too great for us; like it had tonight. If we could make it through tonight, we could make it through anything. I now knew we had the ability to fight this thing, to take care of Matt, because we were not alone, we had each other and more importantly we had the Joshes of the world to help us out. We were soon to find there were hundreds of Joshes out there for Janet and I and our whole family.

As I walked down the hall, I stopped and pulled out my cell phone. I dialed directory assistance and asked for the Mayo Clinic. I wanted to see what options we had, to begin moving forward and seek the best help we could find. I did not want to wait. I wanted to start Matt's recovery right now at 3:00 a.m. in the morning from the hospital lobby. I called the clinic, hoping to get some answers, to schedule an appointment, to do something. The phone rang through and I got an answering machine. The clinic was closed, but I could call back again Monday through Friday during regular office hours. I remember just hanging up the phone and thinking, even the Mayo clinic is of no help to us now! We seemed to be very alone at this point in our lives.

I went home that night to be with Chris and Andrew. They were scared to death and wanted to know what was going on with Matt. I could see the fear in their eyes, and made the decision at that point that we would do everything we could to shield them from the pain and suffering. They did not need to see their big brother suffer. They didn't need to worry about him. They were old enough to understand but young enough that they still needed that safe, secure place in their lives. That place was mom and dad, and home, and we needed to keep this a safe place for them.

After getting a few hours of sleep, I returned to the hospital to join Janet. Matt was still in a great deal of pain and spastic, but the morphine was helping. He continued to hit the morphine pump three or four times an hour and he continued to take shots for the pain every couple of hours. Even this was still providing him minimal relief. We sat that morning in a daze. We knew what the night before had been like, and we knew he could not go through many more nights like that. We began making calls, and talking to everyone we could think of to find some answers. Janet called the doctors she worked with, and called friends and relatives of ours trying to make sure we did not leave any bases uncovered. We wanted to make sure we were not missing anything.

Around noon on Sunday Dr. Miles came to the hospital to see Matt. She had a meeting with some of her partners that day so came to see Matt instead of the on call doctor. Matt's case was already becoming fairly well known. No one had really seen anything like it before. Even when Janet called the doctors she worked with they had researched the symptoms, hearing about the case of the seventeen-year-old boy the hospital was dealing with. Once they heard who it was people began going out of their way to help us find answers. When Dr. Miles came down the hall it was obvious she was going above and beyond the call of duty to take on Matt's case. She had her young baby with her and a fairly young daughter who was babysitting for mom while she made her rounds. I was beginning to understand why Janet was interested in having her as Matt's doctor. Coming to the hospital like this was above and beyond the call of duty. Once there she had a very calm and deliberate sense about her that put us all at ease. Matt liked her from the beginning and seemed to trust her right from the start. She examined him and looked at this chart. She calmly talked with him and let him know the acute phase had passed, and that he would continue to get better now. She began telling Matt how it would go from here, and for the first time, someone was telling him what would happen. She began explaining to Matt what was going on and what would happen next. She reassured him that he was going to get better, but… she also let him know it was going to be a fight, and that it was not going to be easy. She told Matt he needed to stay calm and that he needed to communicate with us and that he would need to do everything he could to fight back. She told him the worst of it should be over, but he needed to be strong and fight this thing. When Dr. Miles finished talking to Matt his attitude seemed to improve, and he began gritting his teeth and digging in. He seemed to realize that the only way to beat this thing would be to dig in and fight the pain.

Dr. Miles ordered some changes in drugs right away. While her goal was still to keep Matt as comfortable as she could, she wanted to try some slower, long-acting drugs to begin dealing with the pain on a more

Graduating With Honor(s)

long-term basis. While Matt wanted to stay as comfortable as he could, he was willing to try some things that might work in the long run even if it did mean a little more suffering for now. We were very pleased with the way Matt related to her, and his willingness to trust her. He seemed to have confidence in what she said, and what was going to happen. He seemed to realize that he was going to be all right. She was obviously a very caring and gifted doctor. From the very start, we realized how fortunate we were to have her working with Matt.

Later that afternoon, a psychiatrist came to visit with Matt. There was concern about how Matt would handle the debilitating aspects of what was happening to him. They wanted to make sure he was able to discuss his feelings about what was going on, and to evaluate how he was handling his illness. The psychiatrist met with Matt for a short time. She told him he was lucky his disease had not progressed any further, and that, in more serious cases, the paralysis had actually affected patients to the extent that they could no longer breath and that he could have ended up on a respirator. She told Matt how lucky he was, and offered to be there to talk with him any time he wanted. Matt responded very little to her. He did not believe he had been lucky, and in all honesty he was still petrified that the pain of the night before would return. At this point, Matt was still too close to the ordeal to talk about it much. For sure, he was not seeing himself as being lucky at this point. He told us he did not want to see *that* doctor again. We took this as a sign that Matt was getting better. He was fighting back, and he did not want people around who did not understand the fight. He had been a healthy high school senior who had been looking forward to cross-country, band and graduation. He did not want to hear how lucky he was to be laying in a hospital bed writhing in pain. Though he was polite, he was also very firm. HE WOULD NOT SEE THAT DOCTOR AGAIN!

Later that afternoon Father Mike came to visit from our church. Janet had called him to tell him Matt was feeling God had given up on him. Father Mike spent some time with Matt, and when he left, the old Matt had begun to re-emerge. He was again ready to fight the pain and get on with this thing. He was in much better spirits and seemed less frightened. Whatever Father Mike had talked to him about had helped to lighten Matt's load. For now, with a little encouragement, we were ready to move on again. We were slowly taking the next steps in what would be a long road to recovery. That night, as the drugs began to wear off, Matt slowly began shaking and feeling more pain. We, again, did not know what to do, but continually tried to reassure Matt that this was part of the recovery and that the pain would be part of his recovery. This time, though the pain was as severe as before, knowing that it was normal for this disease, and that it was normal for what was happening, made Matt more at ease. He panicked less, and fought back more. He knew this was part of the battle, part of what he was going to need to do. He was learning to relax and deal with the pain, rather than panicking. Now if he could only teach Janet and I the trick, we could all handle the predicament better.

That night the first of a long line of visitors began to appear. Josh came back with Jason, Emily, Marizta, Sara, Dave, and Luke. This group started a vigil that would go on with Matt for months. This group was literally his lifeblood. Friends started trickling in one by one, but before long a steady stream of visitors was lined up in the hall. To our amazement, this continued for months, all throughout the time Matt was sick. From one of his long time school friends, to neighbors who saw Matt rarely, the line of people continued. Many had heard about Matt and wanted to see him. They wanted to offer their support and make sure he knew he was not alone through this ordeal. While most could not understand what was happening to Matt, the concern they displayed for him was overwhelming. Whatever their reason for coming, it was important to Matt and to Janet and I that they were there now. We needed all of the support we could get. Even more important, it was important for Matt to know that he was not alone, and that people were thinking of him. To our surprise the site most of them saw when they walked into the room did not phase them. This was especially true of many of Matt's close friends. They did not see the IV tubes or the shaking writhing body, arms filled with needles and bruises. They saw Matt. He was a hurting friend who needed their support right now. They saw the Matt they knew and cared about. Matt's friends formed a vigil around him talking to him and sitting close and holding him. They seemed to know that it was very important for Matt to know that he was not now nor would ever be alone. At times when the nurses came in to work on Matt or change IV's his friends were unfazed. They mostly ignored the nurse's presence and just kept talking with Matt, distracting Matt from the pain and agony he was suffering. They were letting Matt know, in their own way, that it would be o.k. His friends did not see a broken, wounded Matt. They saw a Matt that needed support, and they were there for him. Right now, that was something Matt needed very much; to know others saw him getting better, recovering. This gave him the courage to go on. After his friends trickled out that afternoon Matt was exhausted and still doing all he could to fight off the pain. It was becoming obvious that it would take all of Matt's strength and ours to get through this. Matt's friends also realized the long road ahead of him and they were there for Matt during the next few days to offer their support and encouragement. It was the support of his friends that literally kept Matt going.

Some visitors like Grandpa and Grandma broke down at the sight of the pain and suffering Matt was going through. One of the most painful times of this whole ordeal was watching Matt as he looked in people's eyes and saw the hurt they had for him. Ironically, one of the things that bothered Matt most was the way other people broke down when they saw how much pain and agony he was in. He did not want other people to hurt because of him. Matt tried to be strong when other people came into the room so they would not have to watch him suffer. When we saw how exhausted Matt became trying to be strong for visitors, we began being more and more protective of him. He had enough pain and agony to deal with himself, that we felt he should not be put into a position of worrying about others. For Matt's sake, we slowly began limiting his visitors to those who we thought could handle his pain themselves. Everyone around Matt had to be strong, for his sake.

It was also during this time that Janet and I realized that regardless of how we felt, from this point on, we had to be strong for Matt. We had to have the courage to be strong for him. Janet and I talked about this, and both of us seemed to know the best thing we could do for Matt was to take care of ourselves. That has been one of the most difficult things for us to do, as we have both struggled to stay strong.

The list of visitors that came to the hospital was endless. The calls we received left us awestruck at the outpouring of support we were receiving. We just could not believe the number of people who were willing to share our pain. To help us deal with Matt's suffering. From that very first night while we were scared and frightened, we knew we were not alone.

Josh was without question the rock of Gibraltar for Matt. The depth Josh demonstrated at such a young age was incredible. He and Matt's friends Luke, Jason, Emily, Dave, Sarah, Marizita, Danny and a list of others too long to mention, provided the physical and emotional support that was so vital to Matt during those days in the hospital. Janet and I often joked that we should have created a guest book, so we would know whom to thank. Josh, who had been there during the very worst, had now solicited a group of Matt's friend's who would prove to be overwhelmingly supportive of him through this entire ordeal. We were amazed at how this courageous group of kids went to Matt's bedside and began holding him and comforting him. Without question, these young people were better than any drugs or medicine the doctors could give Matt. Little did we know that the journey we were beginning now would run for months and, that without fail, this group would be there to provide support to their friend "Deal."

That night, as things calmed down again, the Tschetters once again came to visit. This time Lynn, Anne, Jessie and Josh all came. By now, Janet and I welcomed the sight of Josh, as his visits provided us a break from Matt's bedside. When Josh left Matt's attitude and spirit were always greatly improved. Each time Josh came we stole all of the time we could away from Matt in an attempt to recompose ourselves and regain some of the strength it would take for us to stay strong for Matt. The visits from the Tschetters were very healing for all of us. They taught us to pray and to rely on God when we felt like we couldn't go on.

By day three in the hospital Janet and I were on automatic pilot. We were not thinking real clearly and the physical and emotional strain of Matt's illness was beginning to take their toll on us. We were getting very little sleep, and at least one of us tried to be at Matt's bedside at all times. He was still very frightened, and when one of us was not there, he was asking where we were. The visits from people like the Tschetters really seemed to be chances for us to gather ourselves and to gain some rest. Even though it was something as simple as an hour or two away from the room, it was time we needed at this point to hang on.

Before the Tschetters left that night we all spent time praying together again. Ann led us in prayer, her words and prayer continued to help us have the faith and strength to continue on. However, we were still struggling with what was happening.

While the Tschetters friendship has been important to us, from that very first night their faith and their ability to help us keep our own faith has been essential. From that very first weekend Matt has often said he wished he had the same faith and ability to pray that Josh and his family had. Just hearing him say this was comforting to know that he was evaluating his personal relationship with God through this ordeal.

As Janet and I began to unwind at the hospital that night, we continued to make sure every base was covered medically. We talked to everyone we knew, and researched every Internet site and library we could find to find answers about what was going on. What we were dealing with did not sound like anything anyone had really dealt with before. It was similar to a lot of things, but the doctors just could not nail down what this really was. While Matt was initially diagnosed was a severe disabling paresthesis's, the issue at hand was what had caused it and how should it be treated. The more we read the more it reinforced that we were doing everything we should be doing. While that was comforting, it was not making Matt any better.

Janet had spent several nights at the hospital, so I forced her to go home to try to get a real night's sleep. She looked tired and worn; like she was carrying the whole weight of Matt's illness on her shoulders. In some respects, due to her medical knowledge, that was probably more true than we cared to admit. After Janet left for home that night, I took her place on the fold out chair near Matt's bed. I sat there until nearly 3:00 am watching Matt drift in and out of sleep. Chris, Matt's male nurse, was on duty that night shared with me his own story of health problems and how he had pushed through them. It reminded me that there is always hope, no matter how bad things get and that the human body can go through some pretty incredible things. Matt talked about this nurse Chris often during the next weeks. Chris had obviously talked with Matt and provided him the opportunity to see that there was, in fact, a light at the end of the tunnel. Though some of these were very little things, they were just what we all needed to hear. Just to know that there was hope, and that things would get better.

    That night around 4:30 am I was awakened by some noise in the hallway. As I lay there I watched Matt. His morphine pump was making a ticking noise every few minutes then would just click away again until the tick came. Matt was lying with no covers on and his legs propped up in the air. It still hurt to have anything at all touching his feet or legs, so he tried to get his heels just at the edge of a pillow, so as little skin as possible was touching the bed. Suddenly, his right foot moved over and touched his left foot. The next thing I knew Matt was sitting straight up in bed screaming in pain. He began shaking, calling out loud and then he broke out into a full sweat. As I watched his reaction to the touching together of his feet, I could not imagine what he was going through. How in the world could he be in that much pain? I got up and tried to calm him. He hit the pump several times, and pushed the nurse's button for another hypo. It had only been two hours since his last shot, but it was obvious he could not take the pain much longer. He continued to hit his morphine pump, then once the hypo took hold, he gradually fell back to sleep. While I watched him sleep, his legs and arms twitched in constant pain. The best he was able to do was to sleep for a few minutes then the spasms started again. It was almost unbearable to watch.

Daniel D. Deal

Matt in Spearfish Canyon

Josh and Matt warming up

Josh finishing at Spearfish

Matt and Dad at Mile 11

Graduating With Honor(s)

Janet, Sam (hidden), Andrew, Logan & Chris Mile 12

The Deal Crew

Daniel D. Deal

Matt, the cousins and brothers Matt, Sam, Chris, Logan, Halie, & Andrew

Matt Finishing with Mark, Trevor, Chris (on Scooter) & Andrew

Matt finishing in Flandreau

Matt Struggling to finish Laurel O'shea and Ann Tschetter cheering the team

Graduating With Honor(s)

Band Picnic

Matt OG Band
"Horns UP"

Matt "With Pride"

Andrew, Chris & Matt
At the Packers Game the Day his legs became numb

Daniel D. Deal

Deal Boys Relaxing

Chris, Matt, Dad, Andrew

Matt's Senior Picture

CHAPTER 7
RECOVERY BEGINS

The next day was Monday, and life in the hospital changed quite a bit. There were now doctors, nurses, nutritionists, and staff all over the place. During the past few days, it seemed like there had hardly been a soul on the whole floor. Matt had continued to improve during the night as the pain medicine began to catch up, but now he was completely exhausted and just wanted to sleep. The beauty of hospitals is that the timing is never quite right. After being unable to sleep and in great pain all week-end, he was now comfortable and wanted to sleep, only now the nurses kept coming into the room to get him up. As they started poking and prodding at him again, it was obvious it was going to be a long day for us all.

One of the first things they wanted to do with Matt today was to get him up and see if he could walk. They wanted to see how much damage had occurred, and evaluate how much strength he still had left in his legs. They put Matt on a set of parallel bars to see how much weight he could put on his legs and feet. When Matt's toes touched the ground, they curled up into the bottoms of his feet and he recoiled in pain. When they had him try to walk with a walker, he pulled up with his arms and pushed himself along slowly with just the tips of his toes. If it had not been so frightening to watch, it would have been almost comical. He compared trying to walk that day to walking on hot coals with nails in your feet. He said that he felt like he was going to pass out from the pain with each step. Sweat dripped from him with each step, and his legs and arms shook from the pain he was feeling. While the doctors wanted him up and walking around as much as he could, it was obvious that any amount of touch to his feet was excruciating for Matt.

After his trip to therapy, Matt was very depressed. He was in extreme pain, and he was beginning to realize how hard everything was going to be. He was so accustomed to just getting up and walking and the realization that he was unable to do that was devastating. While the doctors still did not know exactly what they were dealing with they felt it was important to try and keep Matt moving. The symptoms Matt was having were not getting worse, but at the same time the pain was not improving either. At one point the doctors questioned whether or not some of what Matt was dealing with was psychosomatic. My concern with this was that even in his sleep he was experiencing extreme pain. How could it possibly not be real? As the doctors struggled to find more concrete answers, it was becoming very discouraging for Matt. He did begin to slowly hold his own with the pain, but we still were not any closer to finding out what had caused all of this. As we have further researched neuropathy, we have found that in nearly every case, the doctors at some point questioned whether or not it is in the person's head, and that, for the most part, doctors know how to treat the symptoms, but not the cause of the disorder. There is also very little agreement in

Graduating With Honor(s)

the medical community about how best to treat neuropathies when they do occur.

The next few days in the hospital were more of the same. Matt continued to be on a lot of drugs, with few answers and a lot more questions. We were still calling Margaret in the attendance office daily and the visits from the students and faculty increased even more. The concern and compassion they had for Matt was unbelievable. Dr. Miles began adjusting Matt's medications to see if we could find some ways to fight the pain while allowing Matt to be more functional. His ability to concentrate while on the morphine and hypos was limited at best, and as this began turning into a more long term recovery, the plan would need to change. The real question was becoming how much pain could Matt tolerate and how much could we push him through the pain. We have found out that this question may take months or years to answer.

By Wednesday, things had not improved substantially, so they brought in a pain specialist and started talking about discharge. The doctors no longer knew what they could do for Matt at the hospital other than control his pain. They were thinking that he might be more comfortable at home, and that if they gave us strong enough drugs, maybe Matt could manage the pain at home. They increased the dosages of Matt's medications and prescribed the heavy-duty painkiller Oxycotin, as a back up for his pain. While they were convinced that Matt would do better at home, Janet and I had no clue how we would manage Matt's pain and immobility alone.

As we looked at the possibility of taking Matt home, we realized how much work was ahead of us. He still could not walk, he was in excruciating pain and any touch to his legs and feet still caused him to go nearly unconscious with pain. While there were drawbacks to going home, we also knew Matt was very tired of the hospital, and that he was not improving at all in the hospital.

CHAPTER 8
GOING HOME

While Dr. Miles did keep Matt in the hospital for a few more days, by Friday he was scheduled to go home. As we began wheeling Matt out of the hospital, I began wondering how were we possibly going to manage him at home. He was still in severe pain, he could not get up to walk, and even sitting in the wheel chair was a major struggle for him as he had nowhere to set his feet or legs. If they could not do anything for him in the hospital, I didn't know what we were going to do for him at home. The days, weeks and months ahead were going to be very challenging for all of us.

Just wheeling Matt to the van and getting him onto a seat was a major ordeal. Trying to lift him in without touching his legs or feet was nearly impossible. He did not have the strength in his arms to lift himself, and his arms and wrists still hurt. He felt like dead weight as we tried to move him. We managed to ease him slowly into the van, where he sat sideways with his body completely doubled over in pain. Once we got him settled in we drove home very slowly. He screamed with pain every time we hit a bump or started or stopped. The two-mile ride home seemed like an eternity.

Once we got home we were confronted with the obstacle of getting Matt up our garage doorsteps, then down twelve stairs to a hide-a-bed couch that sat in the middle of our living room in the basement. This couch would become Matt's bedroom, living room and recreational center for the next several months. We worked to gently carry him up the garage door stairs, then each of us took a leg and carried him down the steps one by one as he used his arms to move slowly but deliberately down the stairs. With each step the jarring and shifting created painful shock waves for Matt that left him screaming in pain. At times we were not sure if we were even going to make it as we carried him down. We had no clue how he was going to be able to manage being at home with all of the pain he was in. After what seemed like an eternity, we got Matt down the stairs and into his wheel- chair. We let him recover for several minutes then slowly moved him to the couch in the middle of the living room. Once there, Matt collapsed in agony, and just wanted to sleep. The trip home had been sheer hell for him and he was shaking, sweating and moaning. Janet and I just looked at each other. We had no clue how we were going to deal with Matt at home. While it had been tough enough at the hospital, the thought of going this alone was terrifying. At least at the hospital we had the nurses to call on when we had to. Now we were completely on our own. And we had only begun!

The first few days at home were sheer hell for all of us. We could not get Matt's pain under control, and it seemed like Janet and I were constantly running to take care of him. Even going to the bathroom was now a major ordeal. We finally realized we had to resort to a hand urinal because there was no way Matt could stand the pain of getting up even a few times a day. From the first day, we quickly learned that everything in Matt's life had to be scheduled around his medications. If we tried anything with him when his meds weren't totally on board the whole day would go down hill rather quickly. We planned everything, even sitting up, around his medication schedule. It was ironic, that even in all of the pain he was in, Matt rarely, if ever, complained. When the pain got too bad he would sweat, spasm, and shake uncontrollably. While we did everything we could to ease the pain, he just seemed to grit his teeth and deal with it.

The next few weeks Janet and I spent all of our time trying to keep Matt as comfortable as possible. We took turns being caretakers for him, knowing that whoever was the emotionally strongest at any given time should be the one to be with Matt. This, in addition to the physical demands of transferring him back and forth to the bathroom, helping him onto the toilet and shower, was very wearing on both of us.

We were fortunate that many of our friends and Janet's coworkers stepped in to help. We were so busy taking care of Matt that many of the things that needed to be done were just not getting done. The help people provided was just exceptional. Lori Mulder, a co-worker of Janet's showed up one night with her husband Eugene. They came and installed handrails down to our basement so we would have something to hold on to when we carried Matt up and down the stairs. Our neighbors, Steve and Lori McGinnis came over and built a ramp for the steps to the garage so we would be able to wheel Matt in and out of the house when the time came. Hardly a night passed without someone knocking on the door with food or homemade meals for our family.

Our neighbor Christa showed up with cookies her mom Shirley had made, another neighbor Marlene came and provided Matt hair cuts all during this ordeal, and believe me, haircuts are a big deal for a sick seventeen year old! We were overwhelmed with the kindness people were constantly showering us with.

While Matt continued to struggle with the pain, day after day it amazed us how well he handled it emotionally. While he got depressed at times, he just seemed to accept the fact that this was the way things were, and that he would just have to deal with it. I do not have a clue how he was able to handle the pain and agony he was in, along with the fear of not knowing if he would ever walk again. We were absolutely in awe of his courage. We did not know how much of it was real, or how much he was trying to hide from us so we would not worry more. During this time we realized Matt was an incredible young man. It was around this time that Matt asked for a shirt with a logo on the back that read "Deal with it." This seemed to be the self-imposed motto he was living by to get through this ordeal.

While the next few weeks were very difficult for Janet and I, it was ironic the number of times we found ourselves comforting people who came to visit Matt. Most just were not prepared to see how he had physically changed. His legs twitched and were spasming a great deal, his feet and toes curled up in a rather grotesque manner, and he was still sensitive to the slightest touch to his legs and feet. He was growing very thin and pale, and the wear and tear of the pain was becoming evident on his face.

I felt as though Janet and I were beginning to age right before our very eyes. I had always been an avid runner, but somewhere in the middle of this my knees had begun hurting so badly I could hardly walk some days. Carrying Matt up and down the stairs or just lifting him into the bathroom was about all of the physical activity I could handle. Janet had a history of back problems and hurt her back somewhere between carrying the wheelchair and carrying Matt. The two of us were quite a sight trying to carry Matt with Janet's bad back and my bad knees.

During the next few weeks we were inundated with people asking what they could do. Janet and I were so tired and so frazzled we just did not know what to do. At times it felt as though I had told Matt's story a million times. I felt as if I had to tell it one more time I would snap. Emotionally, it was taking all we had to be strong for Matt. Telling and retelling the story was very emotional, and not energy we had to expel right now. The very thought of having to talk to people about him was becoming unbearable. While we were trying to be strong for Matt, we were doing all we could just to hang on. We just could not afford to break down in front of him, because that just made things worse for him and for us. I could not count the times during these I would find Janet on the phone crying. She would lock herself into the bathroom or bedroom until she could recompose herself. We were all trying to be strong for each other, but just were not feeling as though there was any end in sight.

The more difficult this all became for all of us the more important we began to realize it was for Matt to be able to talk with someone. If it was this difficult for us to handle things there was no way to imagine how hard it was for Matt dealing with the pain and loneliness of what was going on. Not only was his pain severe, but his disease was so unique that no one could really provide any answers for him. They did not know what had happened to him or why. They did not know why his pain was so severe, or when it would go away. If we were struggling and dying for answers, we could only imagine what was going through Matt's head. This had to be the scariest time of his life.

As time went by the days were now growing into weeks, and weeks into months, yet Matt was not making much progress. The doctors had said he would walk in a week, then in a month then in two months. They pushed for us to get Matt back to school, but with the pain he was in we just did not see any way to make that happen. Matt was having a tough enough time getting through each day doing absolutely nothing. The thought of him trying to get up and go to school was beyond comprehension at this point. Matt continued to fall further and further behind in school. He had missed nearly all of the first semester, and was now in jeopardy of not graduating. He had begun seeing a former co-worker of mine in therapy. Tony Bour was a mental health therapist who I knew to be excellent with kids. He started doing therapy with Matt by coming to our house when Matt was at his very worst. Tony, was again, one of those people who went above and beyond the call of duty for us. In therapy he was telling Matt not to worry about anything but getting well. He told Matt to focus on only one goal, and that goal was getting better, one day at a time. School and everything else would have to wait for now. Matt's full-time job for now was simply to get better. This advice was among some of the best Matt would get. He was able to forget about school, about grades, and about falling behind his classmates. Tony had Matt focus all of his energy on just getting well.

As the weeks passed we realized it was important for Matt to begin physical therapy. In the hospital the therapists had tried to have Matt walk to become desensitized to the pain. As we started outpatient therapy the therapist began with a more remedial approach. The immediate goal would be to simply desensitize Matt's feet and legs to the pain. Matt's physical therapist would work with Matt trying to catch him when he was not looking and grab his feet. If he knew she was going to touch them, he simply would not let her next to them because of the pain.. Matt became so afraid of anything touching his feet or bumping his bed that he would keep his legs curled up under him to protect them. While progress was slow, there was at least some progress. His fingers, hands and arms were slowly getting better, but from the waist down the pain was still unbearable. What was unbearable was not knowing how much longer this would go on, or even if it would ever get better.

We tried to get Matt to do more and more, but for now he left the house only one or two times a week for physical therapy. He did venture out one time to see his therapist Tony, but that had gone so poorly we had to continue to have Tony to come to our house. As we tried to push him to get out more the Tschetters offered an electric wheelchair that would require only the use of Matt's hands. The chair had been Grandpa Tschetter's chair, and at times I am convinced grandpa Ken was looking after Matt. That chair started providing Matt some of the independence he needed to start overcoming his pain.

Up to this point other than his bi-weekly trips to physical therapy, Matt had not been leaving the house. The stream of visitors had now become a nightly thing; lead by Josh, Jason, Luke, Dave, Emily, Maritza, Sarah and on and on. Most nights Matt's friends came and talked, while he just sat and listened. He was finding that it took most of his energy just to avoid the pain. Being social at this point was very difficult for him. He slowly began to try to do a little homework, but the medications had his vision quite blurred so he really struggled with this too.

Janet and I were beginning to get more and more concerned about Matt. We just did not know how much longer he could go on like this. Between the chronic pain and the side effects of the medications, it seemed like he was either hurting or sleeping all of the time. We knew when we could not even get Matt interested in schoolwork there was something very wrong. He had gone months without showing even the slightest interest in homework or school. Janet talked with Matt's therapist Tony regarding how he felt about Matt was putting so much energy into just getting through each day. We were concerned that Matt did not have energy for anything but just surviving day to day. How much longer could this go on? Tony reflected that Matt would only get better as soon as he could, and that until that happened, he could not worry about anything else. He advised us not to push Matt to do anything but get well.

Matt was adamant that he had one goal and only one goal. That goal right now was to just get better. We realized more and more how sick Matt was and we were growing more concerned about his future. This had gone on for months now, and no end was in sight. We were becoming more and more concerned whether Matt was ever going to come out of this.

CHAPTER 9
UP THE STAIRS

As Christmas Vacation neared we knew we needed to do something to help improve Matt's situation. His progress had really reached a stalemate, and Matt had laid in the basement now for nearly a month without coming up the stairs. The pain in his feet and legs continued to be so severe that it took all he could do just to transfer to his wheelchair a couple times a day to go to the bathroom. At this point he was still using a hand held urinal, so was getting up only when he absolutely had to. Janet had taken family medical leave at work so was now staying home with Matt full time. While there was not much we could do for him, he still wanted someone around. He was very concerned he would have a bad episode of the pain again. Since Matt was downstairs and Janet and I had our bedroom upstairs, we gave him a cell phone to call us. I will never forget the first time he called us at 2:30 in the morning for more pain pills. I remember joking to Janet that a lot of parents would love to know where their teenagers were every night. In our case we were praying he could get out and cause some trouble. As the weeks began to turn into months Janet and I were trying to interest Matt in schoolwork. We went as far as reading his books and typing his papers for him. The medications he was on left his vision blurry and he complained that his wrists and arms hurt too much to type or write. We tried to motivate him to keep his schoolwork caught up enough that he would not have to take incompletes for the whole semester. We really believed that once he felt better he would be able to get everything caught up, but with the slowness of his recovery, we just did not know how to motivate him. During this time we began to realize this was going to be a long process and that his illness was something that was going to take a long time to get over. The longer he was a prisoner in our basement the greater the toll it was beginning to have on Matt, Janet, and I. We were also beginning to find that Chris and Andrew were beginning to withdraw more and more. Everywhere we went people kept asking how Matt was doing, and what they could do to help. His illness was becoming the center of our lives, and it seemed like there was nothing we could do to get away from it. The longer this went on, the more we began to isolate ourselves. It just seemed like there was nothing anyone could do, and that dealing with this was taking all of our energy. All we had time for was taking care of Matt, working when we could and sleeping. It was not an enjoyable time for anyone.

During this time the doctors kept telling us to stay positive and to do everything we could to help Matt to stay positive. Right now that was the hardest thing in the world to do. Both Janet and I were walking around in a constant daze. We just wanted this thing to go away and we would all be fine again. The problem was it seemed more and more like this thing may never go away.

For the most part Matt was still just sleeping, hanging out on the couch, and avoiding any kind of physical contact with his feet and legs.

Something needed to change, but we just did not know how to make that happen. The more meds he took for pain, the more he slept and the groggier he felt. If we backed off on the meds he complained about pain, and just could not function. It seemed like a real process of balancing the meds and the pain.

As Christmas neared Janet began doing the normal Christmas things, putting up the trees, hanging the lights etc. I encouraged her to put the tree in the basement near Matt, but she insisted we put it in its traditional location in the upstairs living room. She insisted that s Matt would be coming upstairs for Christmas. At this point, he had not left the basement more than once or twice, and during these occasions we had had to carry him up.

Matt had always looked forward to Christmas, especially the time he would spend with his cousins. This was always a big thing in our family as Janet came from a family of eleven, and every year EVERYONE comes back for Christmas. This includes brothers, sisters, spouses, children, grandchildren, etc. In all, nearly fifty immediate family members gathered together for Christmas. This was always the highlight of the year for the boys, and this year was no different. Matt slowly began talking about Christmas with his cousins, and he began discussing some of the things that he wanted to do.

It was also during this time that we received a call from Josh. Josh told us he wanted to take Matt out to a movie with some of their friends. Josh was insistent that it was time to get Matt out of the house and he talked to Matt and made plans for Matt's first outing. Josh had been over several times in the past few weeks and it was apparent that he was beginning to see how Matt's illness was wearing on Matt and us. While Janet and I had our doubts that Matt could be up that long due to the pain, Josh insisted he could make it work, even if *he* had to carry Matt up the stairs. We agreed to let Matt go, and decided if we loaded him up with his Oxycotin and some other pain pills he would probably do just fine.

When the night of the movie came, Matt showered, got dressed, and then managed to transfer himself into his wheelchair. When Josh arrived Janet and I each took hold of one of Matt's legs and step by step carried him to top of the stairs. While this had to be one of the most demoralizing things in the world for Matt, he was not even fazed as Josh pitched in and helped us by opening doors and moving chairs. We could not believe how well Josh handled these things. He acted like we had been carrying Matt up the stairs all of our lives. Josh's positive attitude and the way he just made things work no doubt affected Matt. Matt was so comfortable being with Josh, that nothing about his current predicament seemed to phase either of them. This was the first time anyone outside of the family had seen Matt be carried, had seen him need a hand held urinal, or seen him shake in pain. Josh was never flustered by any of these things and his attitude allowed Matt to realize he would indeed be o.k.

Thanks to Josh that first night went exceptionally well. Matt had left the house despite the pain! He was shaking, quivering and dying from the pain, but he had finally done something normal. This was a huge step! For the first time, Matt realized he could have this pain, and still live a somewhat normal life. *Thanks to Josh, recovery had begun!*

After that first trip out, the frequency of visits by Matt's classmates increased substantially. Once word got around that Matt had been to a movie, more and more kids began calling and coming over to visit Matt. For whatever reason, they were going out of their way to make sure Matt was feeling included. It was our suspicion that Josh, Jason, Emily, Sarah, and Dave were a large part of this. They had obviously begun recruiting friends to go and see "Deal".

It wasn't hard to see that Matt was beginning to live for the nights that his friends would come over. He had hardly been out of the house in four months, and he was getting lonelier and lonelier. He would nap most of the day so he would have the energy to be up when his friends came over after school. Sometimes they would stop only for a few minutes, but these were very important minutes to Matt. There was a core group of students, Josh, Jason, Emily, Sarah, Dave, Marizita, Luke and Dan that seemed to show up just when Matt needed it the most. With their support he was slowly but surely beginning to make some progress. While Matt's pain was not a great deal better, his attitude had improved, and he was beginning to feel like part of the world again. He began to realize that people were still thinking about him, and still wanted to include him in their lives. We credit the band director Smitty and the staff at O'Gorman with helping to facilitate this by encouraging students to keep reaching out to Matt. While we had no clue what direction Matt's recovery would take, it was important for

him to know that his friends were sticking by him no matter how bad it got.

CHAPTER 10
MERRY CHRISTMAS MATT

As Christmas approached we wanted to use the holiday to bring some joy into Matt's life. We felt as though we really needed to go out of our way to make the holiday special for him with all that he was going through. We were at a total loss as to what we could do for Christmas and he really did not give us have any ideas. The one thing he did look forward to right now was watching the Indiana Pacers games on t.v. As Matt lay week after week on his couch in the middle of our basement he developed an interest in NBA basketball. He started following Mike Miller a local kid who played for the Orlando Magic, and then he began developing an interest in other teams. Matt became interested in the Indiana Pacers and it became a goal of his to see a Pacers game when he could walk again.

While we did not know how we could possibly get him to a game, Janet called her brother Jerry who lives in Indiana to see if he could help us in any way. Even if it just meant getting a jersey or a pair of shorts, anything we could give Matt might help to cheer him up. On Christmas Day, true to her promise, Janet made Matt come up the stairs to spend the holiday with the family. While it took nearly everything he had, Matt did make it up the stairs and to the living room couch. He was still in enormous pain, and was becoming depressed at the thought of having Christmas and the rest of his life passing him by in such a miserable fashion.

As we began opening presents the room was deathly quiet. Everyone in the room was miserable, and we could not help but feel the pain Matt was in. We had all watched Matt suffer for nearly four months, and right now, there was no end in sight. Janet and I were just wishing we could take all of Matt's pain away and make this the best holiday ever.

As we began opening gifts the mood of the room was pretty glum. What we all really wanted for Christmas was for Matt to be better, and that just was not going to happen. Matt seemed to be using every ounce of energy he had to sit up, and he was polite but obviously sad at the Christmas he was having.

As he opened his presents he thanked everyone and smiled politely. As we went around opening presents we came across a box that had come UPS from Uncle Jerry. Matt slowly tore the tape of the box. As he reached in he pulled out a purple and gold banner Pacers banner. For the first time today a twinkle slowly grew in his eyes. He then pulled out a purple and gold Pacers shirt, then a Pacers hat. With each item the smile on Matt's face grew wider and wider. This was the first time in months we had seen him forget the pain. For a minute, he was able to leave the suffering behind. Then Matt pulled out an autographed picture, then another, then another. Matt continued by pulling out a picture of Brad Miller, then a picture of Ron Artest, and then an autographed picture of his ultimate hero Reggie Miller. Matt just screamed "No way!" "Reggie doesn't do autographs"! He was beaming from ear to ear. It was the first time in months we had seen that smile. The boy we knew was back, if only for a minute, he was back! He was excited, and for the first time that day we heard what we have heard very often since and grown to appreciate. "Thank you mom and dad". Thanks to Uncle Jerry and the Indiana Pacers. For the first time in weeks there seemed to be hope in Matt's eyes. While the Pacer players will probably never know it, the time they took to sign those autographs for Matt was the spark he needed. For him, just knowing people of celebrity status took the time to write to him had made his Christmas.

During the remainder of the holiday break things continued to improve. There were more movies, and even a crazy Christmas light tour. Josh and several other students came over to take Matt around town to see Christmas lights. They poured fourteen people in Josh's Durango with Matt propped in the middle of the crowd somewhere. They drove around looking at Christmas lights, singing Christmas carols, and having a great time laughing and being teenagers. Matt had not been a teenager for some time now. The tour had completely wiped him out. He needed extra doses of pain medications, and slept nearly all of the next day. But for Matt, it had been the chance to be normal again, and he needed that.

After Christmas we began to see flashes of the old Matt begin to return. He wanted to start getting caught up in his homework. His teachers had all agreed to give him until the beginning of the next semester to get caught up with his homework and now he began plugging away. As he struggled, he also had to make some decisions that nearly killed him. For the first time in his life Matt had to accept that he could not do everything he wanted to do academically. He had to accept that rather than graduating with a 4.0 and honors, he was going to have to drop several classes, complete the classes he could, and just settle for getting enough classes to graduate. The combination of the pain, and the way he was wiped out half of the time from the medications just gave him no other option. Even by dropping the classes he did not need to graduate, Matt still had a semester's worth of work to do in just a short time. He had a long way to go if he was going to graduate this year with his class. Matt began doing more and more homework each day. He did religion, English and history. At one point he had a paper to write so he dictated it to me and I typed it on the computer. He still did not have the dexterity or hand strength to write well, so he would write a few sentences, then dictate a few sentences, and slowly but surely we produced some papers. I learned early on not to mess with any of his work. One day as he was writing I changed a few sentences in one of his papers and he became very angry with me for messing with his work. I don't know if it was as much frustration with what I had done, as much as it was frustration at not being able to do everything like he wanted to. It was painful to watch Matt try to study like this, at times, he would literally fall asleep with his face in the book after taking his meds. But he was trying, and slowly but surely the old Matt was beginning to return.

As Matt continued studying he was having more and more difficulty reading due to the vision problems his medications were causing. Janet read several assignments for him, but when it came to an assignment to read a major novel, he just knew there was no way he could do it. Janet volunteered to read the book to him, and the school offered readers, but Matt wanted to do it by himself. Finally, like so many good fortunes we were beginning to have, the teacher came up with an audio taped copy of the book. The tapes were nearly twenty-four hours in length, but Matt was committed to doing it himself. We hooked up a cassette player next to his bed, and he began listening to the tapes hour after hour. He had been struggling with insomnia for the past few weeks, and there were several times I would wake up at three or four in the morning and hear him listening to tapes of *Jayne Eyr*, and asking himself questions about what he had heard. At times it was almost bazaar. Here he was in dehumanizing pain, unable to walk, yet at four in the morning here he was listening to this strange voice narrating this book. His motivation and drive were incredible. He was committed to getting back to where he had been mentally and physically, and it appeared he was going to do whatever it took to get there.

Janet's family had planned to celebrate their Christmas holiday the weekend after Christmas at a local motel. As we started packing to go to the motel we realized how difficult it was going to be to take Matt along. He was still unable to touch anything to his feet without going in spasms that left him in near full body seizures. Matt compared the pain to that of being electrocuted, with the shock beginning in his feet then shooting up through his legs and arms.

Graduating With Honor(s)

As we wheeled Matt in his wheelchair even the slightest bump put him over the edge. The trip to the motel alone was about all Matt could stand so he immediately went to the room to rest. Our niece Michelle is now living in Texas and had worked at Baylor University in the Occupational Therapy Department. She had heard about Matt and she was fascinated when she saw him in his wheelchair. Janet had made this contraption for the chair out of blankets and foam rubber to lessen the shock that came through the chair when it hit bumps or went over rises in the floor. He still had his feet propped up in the air to avoid shock, and he was wearing gym shorts because the touch of clothing to his skin still hurt immensely. Michelle looked at Matt's feet and was amazed at how any touch to his toes or feet sent him into spasms of pain. She spent hours talking with Matt about his symptoms, his pain and his physical therapy. She was amazed that they were still trying to walk him, and that they had not found a way to protect his feet to provide him a higher level of comfort. After the first afternoon with him Michelle asked Matt if he would be willing to let her try some things with him. Matt was reluctant at first, but Michelle had some ideas, and wanted to see if they would help him at all.

At first Michelle took a cotton ball, showed it to Matt and slowly approached him with it. First she asked him if she could touch his feet with it and, though he was reluctant, Matt agreed; but only if she touched his toes. Michelle was amazed at Matt's feet. The skin was all cracked and dry and they looked deformed. His toes were all curled up, and his feet were locked in an inward position that made him appear deformed. Matt's feet had not been touched for weeks, not even so much as having them in water when he showered. Any touch to his feet sent Matt into severe pain and spasms. Michelle took hours explaining to Matt that they needed to begin desensitizing his feet. She described what was going on with his nerves. She explained the process of having the nerves heal, and the fact that they then needed to regenerate so they would once again receive messages from the brain. Michelle needed Matt to agree to let her use the cotton ball first to just touch his feet. If he could start there, the goal would be to slowly increase the touch to his feet until they could eventually return to normal touching and feeling. Slowly but surely Michelle took the cotton ball and touched the tips of Matt's toes. The first touches sent shock waves through Matt's entire body. He began sweating and was in unbearable pain. His legs recoiled from the pain, but he was willing to continue. This was the first time in weeks anything had touched his feet, and he was willing to keep at it. Michelle continued very slowly. She touched one toe, then another, then another. She slowly moved the cotton to the ball of his foot, and though he was in agony, Matt allowed her to continue. The first time they went only minutes, but Matt was excited; there was finally some progress. Over the next couple of days Michelle was able to touch Matt's toes more and more. He let her put some oil on the cotton, and began working to get his feet back to normal. This was a huge step for Matt. Someone had touched his feet, and he was willing to let her do it again and again. He was again beginning to realize the pain was part of the healing, and he was going to need to push through the pain. This was going to be incredibly difficult to do.

During the next couple of days Michelle continued to work with Matt and evaluate him. She did not like the way the unexpected bumps to his feet caused him to withdraw, so she discussed with us ways that we could protect Matt's feet so he could begin to have some control over the pain. She did some calling, looking for a special boot for his feet that she used with patients in Texas in her therapy. None of the local doctor's or medical supply stores had ever heard of such a boot, but after several calls, including a call to Baylor University, we were able to order something close to what Michelle recommended. The boots were lined with sheepskin but were completely open, with a big plastic looped heal. They allowed Matt to put his feet in them, but the bottoms of his feet did not touch anything. These boots would allow his feet protection and allow him to keep his feet safe. All of the weight was supported at his ankle. When the boots arrived Matt and his physical therapist Becky were very excited to see them. Becky made a trip over to our house on New Year's eve to personally deliver them. She, like so many people involved with Matt, simply went above and beyond the call of duty.

The boots were exactly what Matt needed. They would prove to be the most important part of his therapy. They allowed Matt to keep his feet safe. With his feet safe, he was now able to begin returning to more normal functioning. He was willing to go places, without worrying about his feet getting hit and starting to spasm out of control. Matt's recovery was to begin in earnest now that he had the boots. He was quite a site in these big sheepskins looking devices, but Matt could care less. They protected his feet, and kept him out of pain. That was his first priority for now.

With his new boots as protection, Matt began venturing out within the next couple of days. After months of being cooped up in the basement, he was finally willing to explore the world outside again, with the help of his new boots. He took a few trips with Janet, then with me, then slowly but surely he began to venture out more and more. A trip with his cousins, another trip to the movie, he had done more in the past week, then he had done in months.

When New Years came Matt had been invited to a couple of parties, but the thought of going had been out of the question, before the boots. While he was reluctant to go, with the prodding of niece Michelle, Matt finally agreed to go to a New Year's eve party. It was funny, but we were probably the only parents in town who were wishing our seventeen year old <u>would</u> go out on New Year's Eve. Michelle even agreed to accompany Matt to the party so Janet or I would not have to. Matt left late that night, not wanting to overdue it his first time out. He was only gone three hours, but he had gone! Thanks to his boots, his wheelchair and his drugs, he was out of the house. This was another big step in his long road to recovery.

CHAPTER 11
BACK TO SCHOOL AND OFF TO THE PACERS

When the holidays ended and Christmas break was over it was time to take the next big step. Matt would need to begin thinking about returning to school. The doctors continued to say Matt should be walking by now, but it was obvious that the pain he was having was still so great, that walking was still a long ways away. How far away we still did not have a clue. But for now, there was no way walking was even a consideration for Matt.

While we were making progress it was slow progress. It still had not really been determined what has caused Matt's illness. The best bet at this point was that he had contracted an autoimmune disease from the mono that had attacked his nerves. The doctors said he had a variant of Gillian Barre that had not affected the muscle, just the nerves. That was good news and bad news. The good news was that he had all kinds of strength. The bad news was that nerves heal very, very slowly, and once they do, they need to be retrained and new pathways need to be developed. This was going to be a long process for Matt, and for us. With Matt's recovery taking so long we were becoming impatient and had begun to do all kinds of research on our own about Matt's illness, his therapy, etc. We found a paper Dr. Miles had written on a patient in the early 1990s with symptoms similar to Matt's. We took this paper and followed up on every reference we could find. We realized the more we could do to find answers the more aggressive we could become in Matt's therapy. Niece Michelle had taught us that if we wait for answers to come they just might not. We were going to have to find many of our own answers if Matt was going to get better. The hunt was on.

As school was set to begin after Christmas break Matt began to push more and more to get his school work caught up, and was showing more signs of his old self. His stamina was still very poor, and this limited him to doing only a couple of things a day. As his first day back to school approached, we knew the key to making his return successful was being able to take advantage of the few good hours he had each day between the meds and the pain. We would have to work hard to coordinate his schedule with his meds. This would prove a tricky thing to do.

Although Matt had been on a few outings, for the most part, he still had been in the basement for the better par of four full months. He could not move very fast, and when he tried to hurry or do more than his normal routine the pain returned rather quickly and he was relegated back to his bed for the day. Janet was beginning to take no for an answer from Matt less and less, and was beginning to push him more. I think we were all realizing that it was now or never. If Matt did not get back to school, he would very likely lose his senior year, and not graduate. A setback like that would have devastated him physically and emotionally.

While it was clear we would have to drive Matt to school everyday, the time was soon going to come when Janet would have to return to work. How we were going to juggle his school schedule, therapy, and our jobs was yet another obstacle we had to face. For the time being Janet had been home with Matt, but once she had to return to work, we were very concerned about what we were going to do. Taking care of Matt was beginning to wear on Janet and I and it felt like we were beginning to look older each day.

On the first day back to school Janet and I took Matt together. We did not know how the physical arrangements were going to work out, so we both wanted to be there to work through the process. Once at school, I unloaded the wheelchair, but from that point on Matt really did not care to have me along. He invited Janet along, but bid farewell to me. I did not know if that was a good thing or not. I watched from the door as he and Janet wheeled down the hall. It was quite a site. He had his furry boots and arm braces on and was wearing nylon sweat pants. By the time we even reached the school he was already in such severe pain that he was shaking and had his head down and was counting his toes. Matt started doing this more and more the longer the pain lasted. He would count his toes over and over to take his mind off the pain. While he knew he was doing it, it was a defense mechanism he was using to deal with the physical and emotional pain. As Janet pushed Matt down the hall I just could not imagine how this could possibly work. He was a mess. He was all drugged up, in physical pain, and totally embarrassed that his classmates would see him like this. I could not believe he was going to go through with it. I was awestruck with courage it took for Matt to let his friends see him like that. The last time he had been in that hallway he had been a blond, tanned runner. Today he was a broken young man in a wheelchair. It broke my heart to watch him go down the hall.

Matt made it only a couple of periods that first day, and it was obvious this was going to be a huge challenge. In addition to Matt being unable to function, the school itself was filled with barriers and was not at all equipped to deal with a truly handicapped person. Since it was a private school, they had done a minimal amount of work with accessibility and the building simply was not ready to deal with Matt and his wheelchair. During those first few days we found that Matt could not use the bathrooms because his wheelchair would not fit. The lunchroom and the office were down several flights of stairs from the classrooms. Eating lunch or even talking with someone in the office were things that we now needed to plan in advance. Even seeing some of his teachers was a problem because many classrooms were not wheelchair accessible. That first day back to school was an interesting one.

When Matt returned home from school that day he was physically and emotionally wiped out. It was obvious that this was more than he had bargained for and he was having second thoughts about whether or not he could really do this. He told us the hardest part of the whole day was all the attention he got. He said the students were friendly, but he just hated being seen like this. A painfully shy person to start with, Matt was totally embarrassed by the attention everyone was giving him.

Graduating With Honor(s)

He wanted to just go to school and blend in like everyone else. He just wanted to be able to do things like everyone else, and he was realizing those days were now gone.

Matt was able to attend even less time the second day of school, and by the third day he was in so much pain, physically and emotionally, that he could not go back. Janet met with the school officials to address some of the concerns we had. The school principal, Mr. Sammons, and the school counselor, Mr. Hegg, took charge of the situation and fortunately for Matt got things worked out. I still believe to this day, if Mr. Hegg had not handled the physical and emotional aspects of what Matt was dealing with, Matt would have never made it through school. The work Mr. Sammons, Mr. Moran, Sister Catherine and Mr. Hegg did to make this happen for Matt was incredible. Mr. Hegg revised Matt's schedule so he would only have to attend half-days of school. He arranged Matt's schedule so that he would be able to be in school when he was feeling his best. He made arrangements, for a restroom facility, and found a place where Matt could park his electric wheelchair at the end of the day. These two also arranged things so as to minimize the attention Matt drew to himself. In short, they listened to Matt and gave Matt the opportunity to succeed within the limitations he was facing. While those first few days back could have easily diminished Matt's spirits, we were fortunate that the school officials went out of their way to work things out and to get Matt back to functioning in school to some degree. Matt really seemed to be digging in at this point, realizing he needed to give everything he had to get through the year. While some of the options were not good ones, they were the only ones we had for now.

CHAPTER 12
ORLANDO

Matt had only been back in school a few days when were faced with our next obstacle. Although this was an obstacle we had created, it was something we still felt like we needed to do to prove to Matt that we saw him as getting better. When Matt had been ill with mono in the fall Janet had promised Matt a trip to see the Orlando Magic play the Indiana Pacers when he got well. We had figured that by January Matt would be well. So in October we had purchased plane tickets to Orlando so we could watch Matt's two favorite basketball teams the Orlando Magic and the Indiana Pacers play. When Mike Miller of South Dakota had begun playing for the Magic, Matt became a serious NBA fan, and begged to watch this team play. Even though we had purchased the tickets some time ago, I had, more or less, written off the trip feeling as though it was more than Matt was able to do at this point. Janet, on the other hand, would not take no for an answer. The trip was on. Everything was paid for and since Matt and his brothers had dreamed about the trip for months, we decided to give it a try. At this point in our lives what could go wrong?

Matt had only been back to school three days when the trip was planned to begin. Those days had not been good ones for him, so we were not full of confidence that the trip to Orlando would go all that smoothly. As a matter of fact, up until the morning of departure, we were still uncertain as to whether or not he would feel well enough to go. Knowing how slow Matt moved, and how easy it was for his day to be ruined by a simple bump or accidental hit, we tried to start very early, and to plan every detail of the trip as closely as we could. As we prepared to leave, Matt complained that his stomach hurt, and that he was feeling weak. I already knew we were going to be in for a long day.

As luck would have it we didn't even make it through airport security without Matt ending up in excruciating pain. Obviously, Matt was not able to go through the standard security check with his furry boots, arm braces, and wheelchair full of paraphernalia. He set the metal detector off and the security guards flocked to him like bees in a beehive. The security guards quickly pulled Matt to the side of the airport corridor. Janet hurried to get through security to warn them not to touch his legs or feet. But by the time she got there they had already removed Matt's boots, bumped his feet and had him in excruciating pain. As the tears streaked down his face, I was angry and wanted to cancel the whole trip. I tried to talk Janet into going on with Chris and Andrew, while Matt and I would stay at home. We were not even on the plane yet, and the trip was becoming a disaster for Matt. Janet left the choice up to Matt, who was really not talking due to the pain, but rather communicating through a series of head nods and shoulder shrugs. He did not give the most convincing nod yes, but for now he was willing to go on.

Graduating With Honor(s)

Due to Matt's wheelchair, we were the first to board the plane. With the trip off to a somewhat rocky start, it now grew more interesting. To get Matt on the plane they had to put him in a skinny little cart and get a special ramp for him. Matt was not sure he could do this because the risk of hitting his feet was very great. He gave it a try and with only slight bumping they were able to get him onboard the plane. Janet was very patient explaining to everyone what had happened to Matt, and why he had these boots, etc. People seemed fascinated by the whole story, and nearly every one we ran into seemed to know someone with the same thing or something like it. It amazed us that none of the doctors or nurses could figure out what Matt had, but the whole world had seen it before or maybe they were trying to make us feel better.

Once they angled Matt onto the plane, we ran into another minor obstacle. The bulk seating on the plane is designated as the handicapped seating area. The only problem is the bulk seating is also by the emergency exit on the plane, so to sit there you had to be able to help other passengers off the plane. They took one look at Matt and realized he probably would not be helping anyone off of anything. The plane was completely booked, but fortunately, some other passengers willingly gave up their seats to Matt so he could get comfortable on the plane. I sat in one seat and he put his legs up on me across the other. The flight actually went rather well considering neither of us dared to eat or drink anything because we knew restroom breaks were completely out of the question.

When we reached Orlando the next part of the trip went rather smoothly. We found our rental van and hauled all of the bags from the baggage claim area to the rental car garage. We had forgotten what it is like to have small children. With Matt being unable to carry any bags, and one of us needing to push him most of the time, that meant one or the other of us was carrying five or six bags at a time. It was amazing though how many people offered to help, and were always helping with elevators and opening doors. It seemed like we were asked a dozen times an hour what had happened to Matt. At one point in the airport he was looking at a magazine when someone interrupted him to ask what was with the boots and everything. For the first time I saw Matt grow impatient. He sarcastically told the women, "Oh, I had a skiing accident". As the woman walked away he just giggled to his brothers and kept on reading.

We arrived at the motel in Orlando without further incident. The motel was nice, but they had not given us the handicapped room as we had requested. They realized Matt was not going to be able to use a regular room. To make up for their mistake they gave us a handicapped accessible room, with a room attached to it for the inconvenience it had caused not having the room ready when we arrived. As we sat waiting for the room Matt got more and more angry. He just hated all of this special treatment and that people kept going out of their way for him. He sooooooo just wanted to be normal again.

Matt was completely wiped out that evening from the long day of travel. It was fortunate that we had not planned anything for the next

Graduating With Honor(s)

day, because about all Matt could manage was a brief poolside visit. He was extremely tired and spent almost the entire day sleeping. The following day, we again had planned to do very little since we wanted to be well rested for the basketball game. We were close to Disney World, Universal Studios and some of the other sites, but we were well aware that we needed to conserve Matt's energy for the Orlando and Pacers game.

We left for the game fairly early, around 3:00 for a 7:00 game. We wanted to make sure we had plenty of time in case we get lost. We wanted to be there to watch the teams' pre game shoot around. We also had no idea what the accommodations would be like for Matt and we did not want to leave anything to chance. As we got to the Waterhouse Arena, hardly anyone else had arrived yet and that pleased Matt very much. The parking attendants saw our handicapped parking sticker and ushered us right through. While we were again receiving special treatment, this time Matt seemed to be very appreciative of everything the building personnel were doing for him. We were able to park very close to the arena. As we began wheeling Matt to the facility we continued to find that people were being extremely nice. The security guards ushered us to a special handicapped entrance, and people everywhere were going out of their way to see that Matt was taken care of. Still we were getting constant questions about what had happened to him.

As game time neared and the doors opened Janet began to talk to the facility people about Matt and his love for the Pacers and Orlando's own Mike Miller. We got to the game in time for the shoot around so

Janet and the boys went down to the floor to see if they could get any autographs. Since Matt could not go down on the floor with his brothers, one of the ushers said she would look into seeing if she could work something out for Matt. That particular usher ended up making Matt's trip to Orlando one of the best experiences of his lifetime! Everywhere we went we kept running into people like this, and it never ceased to amaze us how far people would go to help Matt.

The usher escorted Matt and Janet to an elevator where they ended up in a tunnel that the players went through. She introduced them to a lady named Marsha, who informed Matt that she was the #1 Orlando Magic Fan. She told him that she goes to all of the games, and has the players over to her house all of the time. She showed Matt where to sit to get to see some of the players and as they went by several of the Magic began bantering back and forth with her. Matt was in heaven! As he sat with his mouth wide open, Matt looked up and the next thing he knew he was surrounded by several of the Pacers players and coaches. He is grinning ear to ear as Janet began snapping pictures. He was ecstatic! He got pictures with Pat Burke, Dee Brown, and his favorite player of all time Isiah Thomas. Matt was speechless, not in his wildest dreams did he ever believe this would happen.

Matt returned to his chair and was chirping like a bird. He was on cloud nine. Once the game began it did not serve to disappoint either. The Magic tied the game up with a last minute shot to send it into overtime. The teams battle back and forth in two overtimes until the Pacers went on to win the game on a last second shot. The crowd went wild and Matt was beside himself. He was happy beyond belief. We could not have written this script for a movie and had it turn out any better. As we left the arena I don't think one of us was thinking about Matt's pain for the first time in nearly four months. We were all just so incredibly pumped by the game, the players and the people. It was almost like we were normal again, and that felt real good.

The return trip home went fairly well. The security people at the Orlando airport were super with Matt . They were very patient with him, and took their time to inspect him very slowly. They talked with him a long time, and showed a real interest in his condition. It was becoming increasingly evident that Matt was beginning to be more comfortable with the attention, and was beginning to realize it was important for him to respond to people positively. Many people seemed genuinely concerned, and he was becoming more polite in returning their concern through friendly conversation. It seemed like little things really helped Matt, like the lady in the Orlando airport who came up to him and said she had been in the same boots he had on a year ago. She told him it would get better and hugged him and told him to hang in there. Matt just stared at her as she slowly walked away with her cane in her hand. He was starting to see some light, even if just a dim light, at the end of his tunnel. It was at times like these that I knew God was still watching over us, still making sure we could handle what He had given us, and making sure we still knew that there was light at the end of the tunnel.

We arrived home from Orlando safe, happy and ready for the next leg of the journey. The Florida trip had seemed to build up our confidence that if we could do that with the shape Matt is in, we could do anything. The Florida trip seemed to revive Matt's spirit and ours. Our next goal was for Matt to be walking by his birthday on February 12; a little less than a month away. It was one more goal to shoot for.

CHAPTER 13
BACK TO THERAPY

Once we returned home we learned that Matt's physical therapist Becky was being reassigned and that Matt would be assigned to another therapist. Becky and Matt had been doing a lot of things by trial and error, and while he was not improving as quickly as the doctors had first thought, he was progressing so we were concerned. Even if Matt was making slow progress, it was progress, and we did not want to go in a different direction unless we absolutely had to. We were very concerned that we were losing Becky now. She had helped get the boots, and had moved Matt to the point that he could now get in the water and do some pool therapy. His feet were slowly becoming desensitized, and fewer of his days were being ruined by the severe pain he was experiencing.

When Janet found out that we were losing Becky, she did some calling. She did not want to go through the whole process of doing therapy all over again. She wanted to be sure that we got a therapist who knew what they were dealing with when working with Matt. We had done enough reading on Matt's condition to know that very few people get this condition, and even fewer people had treated it. If we were going to switch therapists, we wanted to be sure we were assigned to someone we could trust, and more importantly someone Matt could trust. Janet knew a few of the therapists that worked for the hospital and requested that they be assigned to Matt's case. As Janet began researching the possibilities she was becoming disappointed because most of the people she wanted were unavailable or did not work with cases such as Matt's. Things were progressing slowly enough as it was. We didn't need to have Matt assigned to a therapist who had not worked with similar cases of nerve damage in the past.

As Janet continued to pursue the options for a new physical therapist a friend of hers recommended someone at the hospital they had particularly liked. Janet recognized the name immediately as our youngest son Andrew's former soccer coach Kim Wieking.

When Janet called the hospital to inquire about having Kim assigned to the case, she was not surprised that he was booked solid and that he was not seeing any new patients. As we had become more and more responsible for Matt's care, Janet had learned that sometimes it was necessary to be persistent and not take no for an answer when it came to Matt's care. This was one of those times, and she was not willing to accept no for an answer and pursued the matter until she had Matt lined up with Kim. She was certain that Kim was just what Matt needed to continue his journey in recovery. From the first time Matt saw Kim, it was obvious she was right. His progress with Kim was constant from that very first day. While there have been ups and downs for Matt since starting with Kim the ups have outweighed the downs ten to one. The extra bonus to this has been that another friend of ours, Mark Bills, also works in the same rehabilitation center as Kim. Mark was usually there when Matt went in for appointments and he frequently helped Matt set up machines and get ready for therapy. The two of them together, Kim and Mark, have done wonders for Matt. Matt will often come home with stories from Kim and Mark. He obviously enjoyed their company, trusted them and was motivated by their conversations with him.

Matt started rather slowly with Kim, but from the first session he was motivated and thinking about getting himself back into shape. Kim had Matt try to walk but did not like what he saw. Matt was on his toes, his feet curled in, and with each step he shook so much that his hips and back were unable to handle the strain. Kim did some internet research on Neuropathies such as Matt had and began to completely revise Matt's therapy. During the next few sessions he went back to working with Matt on desensitizing his feet like our niece Michelle had done in December, and he had Matt begin doing a lot of stretching and isometric exercise. Kim did not want Matt to continue walking in such an unnatural fashion, and wanted to begin working with Matt to build the muscles and tendons that were used in normal walking. He also wanted Matt to begin building up his endurance and to become more active. During their sessions they would work on desensitizing Matt's feet, then at home Matt began lifting weights and working isometric bands along with hours of stretching. Matt had suddenly become motivated to get better and he was beginning to spend more and more time thinking about being healthy again.

As Matt's therapy progressed Kim sent him home with bigger and bigger exercise bands to help him to begin building strength and endurance. Matt started with the small bands by hanging them to the back of the bathroom door. He started with a half an hour each day with those bands and soon progressed to an hour, then two hours. Soon our basement was filled with small bands, medium bands, and finally the mother of all bands', the huge black band. Matt was now doing several hours of this band each day and was becoming extremely fit. There were evenings when his friends would come over and Matt would work on the bands all the while they were there. Sometimes he would work the bands for three and four hours at a time. One night little brother Andrew started playing with the bands and found out how tough they really were. Matt moved his wheelchair as far away from the door as possible to increase the resistance on the bands. He would lock the break on his wheelchair, then proceed to do his exercises. One night when he was finishing his exercises he realized that if he let go of the band it could snap back and possibly break the door. Unable to let go of the bands to unlock his wheelchair he asked Andrew to grab the bands so he could let them go. As Andrew took hold of the band he flew headfirst into the door, banging his head and nearly knocking himself unconscious. We were now beginning to realize how far Matt had really come.

As Matt pushed himself more and more with the bands he eventually overdid it to the point that he began to develop tendinitis in his hands and wrists. This scared him quite a bit because his fingers and hands starting getting numb, and he began panicking that he was having a reoccurrence of his symptoms. Once he backed down from the bands, his hands began to improve, but he was still very cautious. He continued to do everything he could to protect himself and to make sure he was on the right track.

With Kim at the helm Matt began to make great strides. Each time he came home from therapy you would think he had won a gold medal. He was so pumped, so motivated and so sure he was doing things right. What Kim said was gospel. Drink more water, eat more protein; if Kim said it Matt did it. Even on Matt's bad days Kim knew how to get through to Matt and keep him motivated. He told Matt they had to keep talking so Kim would know what was going on in Matt's head even on the bad days. Kim also told Matt even though they did not always agree on therapy, Matt needed to "agree to disagree" so they could keep moving forward and do something. While Kim kept pushing Matt, our friend Mark was always there with his support. He told us one time that this would build tremendous character in Matt, and from the day Mark said it, and gave Matt the idea, you could tell Matt carried himself more proudly. He <u>was</u> going through all of this for a reason, and he was beginning to be aware that a lot of people were watching his progress, and that he was becoming somewhat of a local celebrity. At times he talked about needing to do better so he did not let everyone down that was counting on him.

As things were beginning to improve our neighbor Adam Herther began spending more and more time with Matt hanging out and watching basketball on t.v. One night we were watching a Philadelphia 76s game when they announced that the 76's center, Todd McCulloch would not be playing that night because he was experiencing pain and numbness in his feet and legs and had been diagnosed with a form of Guillain-Barre' Syndrome. They announced that McCulloch had symptoms typical of a peripheral neuropathy and would be out for several games. The announcer went on to add that after talking with Todd he had expressed that not only was it difficult to think about playing basketball right now, but it was very tough even being a human being with all of the pain and numbness he was experiencing. McColloch said just getting through each day with the pain was all he could manage. When Matt heard that story he called me over to the television and said we should get in touch with McColloch. He was excited to hear someone else actually had what he had. This was the first time we had really heard about someone else having the same symptoms. During the past few months lots of people had told us about friends who had had what Matt had, but when we called to check things out it had always turned out to be something different. Matt was excited that he was finding someone with the same thing he had.

Since Matt was so excited I went right to the computer and went into the NBA website. I wrote to the media person for the 76's and asked for more information on Todd McCulloch's situation. I explained that our son had the same thing and we were looking for information about doctors or hospitals that were familiar with this disease and could help us in treating it. Within minutes a reply came back right during the game. The media person gave me the name of Todd's doctor and information on where to find some articles on his condition. I was able to click right into these articles and learned more about peripheral neuropathy in the next thirty minutes than I had learned in the past two months.

The information on the 76's web site lead us to a wealth of information on the topic that not only provided us with the names of doctors, but also to a web site, <u>neuropathy.org</u> and a support group for people dealing with neuropathy. They gave several sources and we were able to print out numerous articles on the disease. What we were learning was that there were very few doctors who had dealt with this condition, but that some had had luck in treating the same symptoms Matt had been experiencing. We learned that Matt had an acute form of neuropathy. The mono virus created the neuropathy when his body turned on his own cells and began eating the myelin sheath surrounding his nerves. We learned that recovery from the disease was dependent on the amount of nerve damage that had been done. No one knew how long it would take for Matt to recover since there was no way they could really determine how much damage had been done. We knew we were on the right track, we just did not know how long this would go on. Just knowing we were headed in the right direction was a tremendous relief for all of us.

Kim continued to grind away at therapy with Matt. They were getting farther and farther down on his feet in the desensitization, but still had at least half of his foot to go. They continued to work on Matt's conditioning, and Matt was now doing warm water therapy on a regular basis. We found a lifeguard at the Wellness Center who was more than accommodating in helping Matt to get pool time on weekends. As the story developed we found out she was a former O'Gorman graduate. She, like so many people, was going out of their way to help Matt. Everywhere we went we kept running into this kind of help. We were still telling friends there was nothing they really could do, but they kept asking and delivering. We were still being swamped with calls, meals, gift certificates and the like. People were simply amazing in their show of support.

The word about Matt's illness was getting around town. Father Mike had continued to come and see Matt, and prayed for him often in church. The meals and visits increased to the point that we were becoming embarrassed with all of the gifts we were getting. Karen Cox, a friend we had from church, came with home-cooked meals and soon became Matt's favorite cook with some of her special dishes. Gift certificates and movie rental cards came by the dozen. People were apparently aware Matt was watching a lot of videos during his recovery. The more the gifts came, the more Janet and I were embarrassed by all of the generosity, but were soon to find out that it was only the beginning. We found that Matt was catching the eye of the whole community. People just wanted to do more, and saying no was "no" longer an acceptable answer to them.

CHAPTER 14
NOBODY EVER HAD A RAINBOW…
UNTIL THEY HAD THE RAIN,

As Kim worked with Matt things continued to improve daily. I could come home from work and literally see the progress with Matt from the day before. We were very excited about his progress, and were feeling very positive that Matt would be walking soon. Then I was at work one day feeling very positive that we were on the road to recovery when the phone rang. Janet was in tears. She was crying and needed me to come home. She cried "He has given up, Matt has just given up." I asked her what she meant and she just said, "come home!" When I got home Janet was outside crying. She said Matt no longer wanted to go on. He did not know if he could do it any longer. He did not want to go to school, he did not want to go to therapy, and he was just through. When I went in the house I saw a very dejected Matt sitting on the couch. While he had fought a valiant battle for the past five months, he was done. He said he just did not think he could fight the pain any longer. He was tired, he was sad, and he was not seeing an end to the hurt. He just cried, "Dad, I can't do this any longer!" I had no idea what to say. He had fought a brave battle. He had never complained and he had been much braver than we could ever have asked of him. I didn't know what to say. All I could think of was that I needed to be strong. I needed him to know that he could not quit, and that we would NOT let him quit.

As I talked to Matt I tried to be compassionate, but I also became angry. We all had invested too much for him to quit now. I told Matt that we were all tired, but none of us could quit. I was tired. His mom was tired. His brothers were tired of having to help all of the time… but not one of us had the right to give up. Matt said did not know if he could continue on. I screamed at him that he did not have a choice, and that quitting was not an option. None of us were going to quit. We just had to go on. By this point, Janet had composed herself enough that she came back in the room. I told her that it was not an option for Matt to quit. We all had too much invested for him to even think about not fighting on. I told both Janet and Matt that now we needed to be even stronger for each other, no one was going to give up! At that point Janet told me to leave, and she started talking to Matt about what we needed to do.

Janet called Tony and Father Mike that day. She got Matt to see both of them, and by the time Father Mike left he told Janet Matt would be ok. He was better now. Father Mike is one of the most positive people we know. He was able to reach Matt and to help him to find strength in God. All of us understood how important God was in all of this. And it was becoming more and more clear that to continue this fight, we would have to continue finding strength through our love of God. While we had not been able to attend church as much during this time due to everything that was going on, we did find ourselves moving closer to God.

It had been interesting to note that through this whole ordeal people continually thanked us for allowing them to help and to be there for Matt. They all talked about how Matt has been such an inspiration to them, and left them impressed with his ability to keep on fighting despite the incredible odds and adversity. While Matt tried to remain positive, the number of times he felt truly despaired could be counted on one or two fingers. To his credit, Matt had accepted what had happened to him and calmly and steadily moved forward. He has never bitten off more than he could handle, and seemed to know how much he could push, and how much he could take physically and emotionally to get well. Father Mike wrote the following poem that beautifully describes the battle Matt has gone through during the past year. We were impressed that these were his observations of Matt through this whole ordeal.

Father Mikes Poem,

The more it hurts, the sooner I walk

Silent growth in darkened womb

"fashioned in secret," or so our

Scripture says; a body formed

For life and Spirit's power

Bursts forth, crying into light.

Muscle and blood, bone and flesh,

A vessel worthy of God where

Daniel D. Deal

Heaven and earth might mesh.

From infant to youth to young

Man, the silent growth of

Flesh and spirit produce

An evolving gift to love.

But a body may weaken,

Muscle betray, flesh rebel

And legs, born to walk and run,

Become a prison cell.

Yet, infants learn with each

Step, faltering and slow,

To find a strength for

Another step and show

the world that a new man,

Strong and free, arrives.

And so we learn, now and

Throughout our lives,

That strength is not always

In those who can train

And compete, but sometimes in

Those who take a step in pain.

and as you replace legs that walk

for wheels that turn,

if we have eyes and heart, we

can see a lesson learned;

and we'll try not to forget,

as flawed people sometimes can

that in his weakness Matt

showed us how to be a man.

Mlg

May 2003

As we continued to push onward with Matt, the hardest thing was trying to figure out what we should be doing and what should come next. The doctors kept saying Matt would walk by this date, then that date... and on and on. Thanks to the articles we had found, we knew that this was a very individual thing; but it was easy to become discouraged with how slow the progress was. That was one thing I think Matt really appreciated about Kim; was that Kim never set dates or time frames for Matt. Kim was very firm in the fact that Matt would walk again and get back to normal, but that would be up to Matt and an ultimate higher power. Kim always seemed to impress on Matt that nobody knew for sure when Matt would walk again, but for whatever reason God's higher plan for Matt was not being revealed. We would just need to be patient and let God's plan unfold for Matt. Kim took it on faith like Ann Tschetter that this had happened to Matt for a reason

Daniel D. Deal

and that God had His own plan. All Matt or any of us could do was to work as hard as we could within that plan for us. Finding the strength to do this took all of the faith we had in God.

An interesting thing that Matt did during this whole ordeal was to never set goals for himself about when he would walk again. While the doctors had set goals for Matt, they had told him he would walk by Thanksgiving, then by Christmas, then before our trip to Florida, then by Easter. While none of these goals were ever met, Matt kept plugging away. While not meeting these goals bothered Matt, he seemed to know that his recovery had no (time table), it would come when it came, and we would just need to be patient. We just could not believe how patient Matt was. As we watched Matt make slow, but steady progress, it was obvious to us that this would be an extremely long process. We remained confident Matt would walk again. His progress continued to give every indication of that, but the struggle was becoming a long and slow process.

CHAPTER 15
HAPPY BIRTHDAY

The next goal that had been set for Matt was for him to walk by his birthday. We did not think that that would happen, but the conversation continued that this would be a nice goal for Matt. He seemed determined to push toward this, but we just did not see how he would come around that quickly. Matt's birthday is February 12, while his brother Andrew's birthday is February 19. As both their birthdays neared, we began planning parties and asking them what they wanted for their birthdays. Matt responded simply "to walk!"

This was going to be Matt's eighteenth birthday and Andrew's twelfth. Janet had always made a big deal out of the boys' birthdays, but as they got older that got tougher and tougher to do. The days of taking them to a restaurant with games and a pizza-delivering robot were about gone. Andrew wanted a few friends over and to go to a movie. Matt did not really know what he wanted to do, but kept saying he hoped his eighteenth birthday would be special. We talked about things he wanted, a new computer, new clothes, etc, but nothing really seemed appropriate. In the past we had tried surprise parties for him but right now it just seemed like we needed to do more for him. It had been such a miserable year. We just wanted his eighteenth birthday to be special for him.

As the day of his birthday neared we could not decide on anything to do, so we decided on a surprise party. We thought possibly that we could get his friends to come over and that would help to make his birthday special. Janet took charge of the party doing everything she could to make this birthday special for Matt.

As Janet went about the birthday planning she put a great deal of pressure on herself to make this a truly special birthday for Matt. He had been through so much, that we just wanted for him to feel better and to be able to enjoy life a little bit. As Janet was struggling with planning to make this a "special" party she bumped into Matt's band instructor Mr. Smith "Smitty." She took this opportunity to tell Smitty about Matt's party and to see if he could help spread the word to some of the band members. Matt had always enjoyed band, and had made many great friends there. One of the things he was saddest about this year was not being able to participate in the marching band. When we had signed Matt up for band as a freshman, I remember Smitty saying that the band room literally became a second home to the band kids at school. This had been the case for Matt as he spent a lot of time in the band room before and after school just hanging out. He was missing these kids, and even on our trip to Florida he had lamented how much fun he had had at Disney World as a freshman on a band trip. When he had contracted mono Matt had insisted we take his trombone in to be chemically cleaned so that when he started to play again he would not be exposed to the germs again. Little did he know at that time that band was over for him for the year.

Graduating With Honor(s)

Smitty's idea of spreading the word for Matt's birthday party was posting the birthday invitation in the band room and announcing it to the whole band. One of the students told Smitty he could not do that because EVERYONE might show up to the party. Smitty responded, "Good. The more the merrier. Then Matt will have a great big birthday party." Word of the birthday party spread quite rapidly. As we went about the community, we kept running into parents who had heard about the party. With all of the attention Matt had received people we didn't even know kept approaching us and asking how Matt was doing. We literally could not go out in public without someone acknowledging that we were the parents of the boy with that rare disease. Everywhere we went this began to follow us. If we wrote a check in the grocery store people would ask what had happed to our son and how he was doing. It had gotten to the point where I really did not want to talk about it at all. I just wanted my son to get better and for people to quit asking. Janet was much better about it and she must have told the story over a million times. She patiently told the same story over and over; how he had gotten mono, how the mono had grown into an autoimmune disease. That the disease had attacked the nerves around his spinal cord, and when those nerves were damaged it left him in severe pain and unable to walk. It amazed me how she could tell the story over and over, reliving the emotions of the past few months over and over. Her patience with people was beyond belief. Everywhere we went people asked, and at times she would retell the story three or four times just as we shopped at the grocery store. She was just so appreciative of everyone's kindness and felt she owed it to people to tell them the story and to update them on Matt's recovery. Some friends like Jenny DeBoer, Pat Everrett and Brenda Ordal probably heard the story too many times.

The day of Matt's actual birthday was during the middle of the week. Since we did not think many students would be able to come then, Janet hedged her bet and planned the party for the Saturday night before his birthday during a basketball game. Her thought was that fifteen or twenty of the pep band kids would probably come over anyway, so if nothing else we could just plan the party for that time. When the night of the party arrived Janet had prepared with cases of soda, bags of snacks, party balloons and the rest of the traditional birthday party favorites.

The night of the party the doorbell began ringing very early and did not quit until late into the night. Student after student arrived asking if this was where Matt Deal lived? Students arrived alone, in pairs, and in packs of five and six. They came early, late, and stayed for hours. Our basement was filled with nearly a hundred kids. Cars were parked up and down the street for blocks. Kids showed up that Matt had not hung around with since grade school. He just sat there through the whole thing with a great big smile on his face. He now realized, more than ever, that he was not alone fighting his illness.

While we have no real idea of how many people showed up that night, we know that dozens of students and even "Smitty" himself showed up. Matt's birthday was another big step in his healing; both

Graduating With Honor(s)

emotionally and physically. Matt needed to know people cared, and we knew that this show of support was important to his recovery.

CHAPTER 16
WE ARE GOING TO DO SOMETHING FOR MATT!

As February began to slip into March, our moods became more subdued as the reality that Matt was probably going to spend his senior year in a wheelchair began to sink in. Therapy continued to go well, but slow. Matt's progress was good, but very slow. As February slowly slipped by and became March we were looking for new ways to divert Matt and to give him something to look forward to. While this is a difficult time of the year in the Midwest anyway, being isolated and in pain in our basement did not help matters for Matt. The winter months were becoming very long and boring, and the days were becoming a grind. Matt was doing well and had put himself in the mind set that he was now going to school everyday come hell or high water. He was beginning to get into a pattern of grind, grind, and grind. He would stay up with insomnia until two or three in the morning, drag out of bed and to school at eight, come home at noon, catch a two to three hour nap, then catch a basketball game on television at night. The next day he would start the whole process over. Matt was still bound to his wheelchair and at this point was still not standing. The goal in therapy was to get rid of the pain before he stood, and for now, the pain was still too severe to consider even standing.

Matt's schedule had been much the same since he had returned to school in January. He was committed to dragging himself to school no matter how bad he felt. Though he struggled to get up each day and was nearly always groggy due to all of the medications he was on, he was very committed to going to school. He had been in this routine for some time when I dropped him off one morning, only to have the school call me as soon as I reached work. Matt was in the school office saying he needed to go home right now. I was nearly panicked. As committed as Matt was to going to school, something real serious must be wrong or he would not be asking to leave. I rushed to the school and ran to the attendance office with my heart in my throat. I kept thinking that Matt had gotten up this morning and had had a really good morning. WHAT COULD HAVE POSSIBLY HAPPENED? I was a nervous wreck.

When I got to the school office, Matt was sitting looking very sad and dejected. He had his head down with his hands covering his face. He looked like he wanted to cry. This was the first time I had seen him like this in public, so I knew something was seriously wrong. When I asked what was wrong he just shrugged and said he needed to go home. As he drove his wheelchair down the hallway it was clear he did not want to talk. As I loaded his chair into the back of the van his head shrank even further into his hands. I was deeply concerned about what was going on. He looked absolutely miserable.

As we drove home he slowly began talking. He told me when he had gone to the office this morning to get his electric wheelchair, one of the students dad was there. He said the teachers were all hugging the dad and they were all crying. Matt said this man got on the school public address system and asked the students to pray for his daughter Andrea. She was a student at the school and a top gymnast. The previous night during gymnastics practice she had fallen and injured her neck. She was paralyzed from the waist down. They did not know if it was permanent or not yet, but her dad asked that everyone pray for her. She was to have surgery that day and he wanted everyone to know how important their prayers would be to their family. Matt was totally beside himself. He did not know why things like this kept happening. He asked, "Why did God let these things happen?"

Matt was totally out of sorts the rest of the day. I kept telling him to pray for Andrea, and that what had happened to her did not affect him. All we could do was to ask God to watch over Andrea. Matt could not seem to get over it, and he asked if he could see his therapist Tony that day. Matt had struggled with many things during the past few months, but for whatever reason, this incident was more than he was able to handle. He just could not stand to see other people hurting. Maybe it was due to the pain he was experiencing himself, but for whatever reason, he was totally beside himself.

This was, in many ways, a turning point for Matt. He was learning that he was not the only one that bad things happen to, and he watched as Andrea fought her battle with strength and courage; it only made him more committed to handle his own suffering with dignity. She became an inspiration for him, and as he watched her courageous struggle he became even more committed to win his personal battle.

Graduating With Honor(s)

By now it seemed the whole community knew about Matt, and everybody wanted to do something for him. The phone calls were continuing. This had now gone on for months. People kept asking what they could do, and if we needed anything. All we wanted was for our son to walk, and for their prayers. We already felt like people had done too much, but the offers just kept coming and coming.

At this point Janet and I figured we must have looked pretty worn, because the offers were growing in number and in intensity. People were still sending food, gifts, and money. No matter how much they did, most people still wanted to do more. Every time I went into a local grocery store there was a young girl named Rosa who asked me how Matt was doing. She always told me to say hi to him. She told me that they prayed for Matt everyday, and that they all wished there was something more they could do. One time while I was writing a check at a local hardware store the clerk asked me if I was related to the boy who had gotten so ill. I was amazed at how the community was responding to our plight.

It was during this time that Matt began making some important strides in therapy. The work Kim had been doing with him to desensitize his feet was now reaching a crucial point. Kim had now moved below the center of Matt's foot and was now nearly able to touch Matt's heels. This had been the very worst part of Matt's feet. As Kim slowly but gently slid his hand towards Matt's heel, Kim kept telling Matt to just let him know when he was ready and Kim would grab on. This would be a huge step in Matt's therapy. As this slow but steady progression continued, Matt went to therapy one day and told Kim today was the day. As Kim moved his hand toward the bottom of Matt's foot Matt prepared himself for the pain, and they let it rip. As Kim grabbed Matt's heal with his hand Matt's legs began jumping in a wild frenzy. Kim kept trying to hold on like a cowboy riding a wild bronco. Matt kept kicking, Kim kept holding on. Anyone entering that room would have roared with laughter. Here was Kim with his hands holding Matt's feet and Matt kicking wildly in the air. It looked like some kind of crazy game. The significance of what was going on was very important to Matt's overall recovery. When it was done Matt was soaking wet with sweat, was in awful pain, and was grimacing. But his feet were now nearly completely desensitized; we could now begin to think about Matt walking again.

When Dr. Miles read in the chart that Kim had touched Matt's heals it apparently struck home how far Matt had come, and how far he still had to go. During our next appointment with her, she advised us that she wanted to have us go to the Mayo Clinic in Rochester for a second opinion. While everyone felt things were progressing nicely, she still wanted to make sure that we were not missing anything. She felt that they were the experts, and they could give us a second opinion on what we were dealing with. She also recommended that we see a doctor of physical rehabilitation that could see if there was anything we could do to that would allow us to be more aggressive in Matt's care.

Within a day or two of Dr. Miles scheduling the appointment at the Mayo Clinic we got a call from our good friend, Karen Dole. Karen said several friends of ours, herself, Karen Johnson, LeAnn Sawyer and

Ann Tschetter had gotten together and decided they were going to do a benefit for Matt. She said they were not really asking our permission to do the benefit, rather they were asking our permission to use Matt's name and the facts about his disease on the radio and in ads. They had been talking and felt it was time that they to do something for Matt. They knew we thought people were already doing enough, but they wanted to do something more for Matt. They wanted to show him how much people supported him. I remember when Janet told me what they wanted to do. We just sat down and cried. While we never admitted it, I think we were both feeling overwhelmed by everything and just the thought of having people come to our aid was a very good feeling.

Daniel D. Deal

The Wiebelhaus Family Christmas

Matt smiling at Christmas

Andrew, Matt and Chris with Matt's boots

Matt's Pacer Presents

Graduating With Honor(s)

Matt boarding the plane for Orlando

Matt with Magic's Pat Burke

Matt with Darrell Armstrong

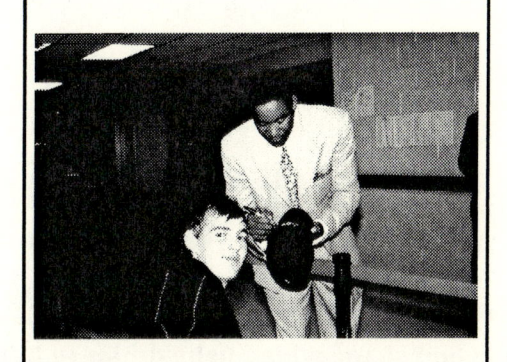

Matt and Isiah Thomas

CHAPTER 17
A TRIP TO THE MAYO CLINIC

The appointment at Mayo was only a few weeks away. As we began looking ahead to it, we had several things to do to get all of Matt's medical records and history together. In the meantime, Matt was continuing therapy, and one of the things we were supposed to do before we went to the Mayo Clinic was to have an appointment with a rehabilitation doctor. The thought was there was possibly something we could be doing in the meantime that would help speed up the therapy process. Janet took Matt to the doctor and they talked about Matt's progress at length. He was impressed with the therapy Kim had done and the way he had not only desensitized Matt's feet, but also that Kim had worked with Matt to strengthen the muscles he would use to walk once we got him back on his feet. Kim's approach was not only helping Matt to get ready to walk, but it was also keeping him strong and in good shape which helped him to handle things better emotionally. The rehabilitation doctor looked at this and offered the suggestion of having Matt undergo an epidural block to take away all of the pain in his feet. The theory was that if Matt did not feel the pain, he would be able to get up and walk. If Kim's theory about having enough leg strength was right, once the nerve pain was gone, Matt should be able to walk.

Everyone seemed fine with this plan, especially Matt who was more than ready to get up and go. While Kim did not discourage the plan, he talked over all of the options with Matt that were available. While the progress they were making was slow, it was still progress. As we talked the plan over at home, it was very exciting to think about the possibility of Matt walking, and walking soon. As we discussed the plan, and as the date for the block neared, we began have second thoughts. We were a little afraid that everything we had worked for might go down the drain if the block did not work. If nothing else, we talked to Matt about waiting until we went to the Mayo Clinic before we made such a decision. By now I had a fairly nice sized library built up from the internet on neuropathies and no where could I find any discussion about such a course of treatment. Most articles discussed the importance of pain management, physical therapy and the use of several medications for people with neuropathy. But nowhere was there any discussion of this kind of an approach. As we considered the options, we knew that the course we were on was a good one. Progress was slow, but it was progress and to attempt anything too radical at this time might backfire. We made the decision to wait until we went to Mayo to try anything too different.

While we waited for the Mayo visit, the planning for the benefit continued. Karen Johnson, who herself is in a wheelchair and fighting M.S., talked with Janet often. She talked not only about the benefit, but also about Matt's treatment, medications, and an alternative diet we could try. Karen gave us advice about diet, and medications. She was the one who got us up and moving toward the Mayo Clinic. Karen convinced us to keep reading and asking questions until every stone had been uncovered. She told us to keep looking around until we were satisfied everything had been done that could be done. She was one of the people who reminded us that if Matt was going to get better we were going to have to keep directing his care.

Karen Dole and LeAnn Sawyer were like two busy bees working on the benefit. LeAnn had married my college roommate Merlin. He had been in our wedding and I had been in theirs. We had been friends since 1978, and though at times we do not see each other for months at a time, they were among the first there when we needed help with Matt. Karen had gone to college with Janet and I had met her husband Kevin through Merlin when they had worked at the same accounting firm. Together we had started an investment club nearly twenty years ago, while our wives started monthly Bunko games. These friendships have run a long time, and for us, they have proven to be the kind of friendships that you want to have. In addition to this group, Ann Tschetter was involved in helping with the benefit. Janet and I counted our blessings very often that we were fortunate enough to have friends like these.

As Matt's illness progressed I was often reminded of the movie, <u>Six Degrees of Separation.</u> The premise of that movie was that six other people only separate each of us from every other person on the earth. In essence there are very few people on earth who are not connected in some way or another. As Matt's illness unfolded, we found people were helping because they were connected to people we knew. As word of his plight spread, the support for Matt was overwhelming because of all of the interconnectedness of our community. Despite the size the city, we could not go anywhere where someone didn't know our story. It was overwhelming.

The following three or four weeks were a blur. We made the decision not to have the epidural block for Matt until after we went to the Mayo Clinic. The benefit was to be a pancake feed organized by the local Knights of Columbus. It was being held the Sunday after the Mayo clinic visit. This could be good or bad. If the Mayo clinic visit went well we could be home and continuing with Matt's therapy. If it went poorly, we may still be at the clinic and would miss our own benefit. In light of everything that was going on, we really hoped that we could be at the benefit. We felt that both Matt and the rest of the family needed a bit of a boost right now.

As the day neared for the appointment at Mayo clinic, I began reading a prayer Ann Tschetter had said for Matt at her church back in October when all of this started. We had posted the prayer on our refrigerator, and right now it seemed so pertinent to the things we were going through. I would find myself stopping by the refrigerator a couple times a day reading different verses of the prayer. Each time I felt as though I was looking for a new source of strength to get me through the day. As I read the prayer I could not help but think back on how far we had come, yet realizing how far we still had to go. The prayer, still posted with a magnet to our refrigerator goes as follows:

MY PRAYER FOR YOU
OCT 20th, 2002

Lord, I thank You so much that You love Matt Deal. You created him uniquely. You care for him deeply. You have a good plan for his life. I thank You that Matt believes in You, trusts in You to forgive his sins, seeks You to lead his life.

We are praying because we care for him too. We pray for physical healing because You are the Great Physician. Heal his mono. Bring him strength and rest. Give him hope. Help him know You care and are there with him. Heal his frustrations as well. It seems so unfair. He works so hard. He sets high and good goals. Yet this illness is out of his control and it sets him back on achieving those goals. Help him deal with this disappointment and frustration… even if he complains to you…You will hear him. Touch him deeply Lord. Develop in him those things that don't come when everything is easy. Build in him the character that only comes when we go through things that are hard. Build in him Christ-like character. Meet him in peace, patience, kindness, goodness, faithfulness, gentleness, self-control." (Gal.5:22) Develop endurance and perseverance in (Roman 5:3-5)… and give him hope…assure him of Your life. Draw him to pray…and answer his prayers. Draw him to Your work… and speak to him there. Help him to Become all that You are calling him to Become… and then Do all that You are calling him to Do. Bring healing to his body. Help him get his schoolwork done well. Grant him health and joy for the rest of his Senior Year.

We thank You too, for Janet and Dan. Thank You that they love You…trust You. Give them wisdom in what to do for Matt and in what to say. They love him so much. Bring healing to their emotions too.

We come to You because You hear us, and You care. In all areas of life...we totally need You. You are hope and salvation in this life...and in the next. We love You.

We pray these things in the precious and powerful Name of Jesus...In the Name of the Father, the Son and the Holy Spirit. Amen! With Love, Ann Tschetter

The beauty of this reading for me was that back in October when we had started this journey, it was a different journey than we have ultimately ended up on; but the prayer and our needs were much the same. While we have struggled long and hard during the past several months, each time I read this prayer I realize how well we have weathered, how strong we have become, and how blessed we have been to have had the opportunity to walk this path with Matt. While this has been a tragedy in many respects, the prayer has been answered. We have been touched, the character has developed, and we have been drawn to God's word. Each time I read this prayer I become more grateful that Matt is loved and that we are all loved and that this love has produced more healing than people will ever know.

Despite weeks of waiting the trip to Mayo finally arrived. What I thought would be a relief really turned out to be the opposite. As the trip got closer, the more our fears grew. We began realizing that while the chances were good that they would not find anything...chances were equally as good that they might discover something new and that we would be starting this whole process all over again. As the day of Matt's appointment neared our nights became more and more restless. I don't think Matt slept at all those last few nights, and Janet and I had

not been sleeping all night for months. It all just worsened as the trip neared.

We were lucky that my mom, Goge, was able to take care of Chris and Andrew while we were away. As the appointment neared it was obvious they were concerned too. They both had begun spending more and more time with Matt or near him. One of them was almost always in the room with Matt either playing on the computer or watching television with him. In their own way they needed to be as close to Matt as possible in case something happened. They had begun making a home for themselves near Matt's bed. Other than school and required activities, neither of them did much outside of the house. They seemed real intent on just spending time in the basement, just watching basketball and being close to Matt. We again, realized how Matt's being sick had really changed our own family. Chris and Andrew had been real troopers through this whole ordeal, and not once did they complain at all they had to sacrifice due to Matt's illness.

Since our appointment at Mayo was very early in the morning, we left the day before and stayed overnight in a motel room. Moving Matt around was still difficult, but his pain was getting better so it was becoming easier to travel with him and to move him around. Despite all of us being rather nervous, the trip to the clinic was quite enjoyable as it gave Matt, Janet and I a chance to sit and talk, and to compare notes on where we were at with things. While we were all nervous, it was good to get Matt out of his normal routine and to give him something to look forward to. We were just praying things would turn out well at the clinic.

I don't thing any of us slept that night. We were up very early and ready to go. The adrenaline was pumping and we were all excited about the day ahead. The hotel had a shuttle to the clinic; which Matt was a little reluctant to ride. Matt still was not comfortable being in a wheelchair and was embarrassed whenever anyone had to help him. He was panicked at the thought of riding the shuttle bus, but surprisingly he did not balk at going on the bus once it was time to leave for the clinic. Like always, two or three people on the ride to the clinic asked Matt what had happened and why he had the boots and was in the wheelchair. As I listened to him tell the story I was proud at how well he was handling himself, and how well he talked to people about his disease. He was really growing and maturing through this ordeal. He was fast becoming a young man of character!

As we walked into the Mayo Clinic for the first time we were overwhelmed. The lobby was huge. We arrived quite early in the morning, so there were very few people in the lobby and it was extremely quiet. We stumbled around for a few minutes, and then found the main counter where you check in. There were six or seven lines with people going through their registration. Matt was obviously feeling a bit overwhelmed, and you could tell he was feeling sorry for us; the worry was no doubt showing on our faces. I am sure Matt was aware that both Janet and I were stressed to the very limit, and he was beginning to apologize all of the time to us. He kept saying he was sorry, and he kept trying to do more and more on his own. We realized how hard he was trying and how hard it must be for him. How was he handling all of this so well?

Once we registered, we headed directly to the department Matt's appointment was in. We were planning to get there and wait, but we wanted to make sure we were in the right area first. We were to see a neurologist who would review Matt's records, visit with us, and see what they could do further for him at this time. Our appointment was at 10:00 and I remember arriving to the appointment area about fifteen minutes early, making sure we didn't get lost and miss anything. The woman at the check in counter apologized because they were running behind. By now we were getting used to clinic appointments so we all drug out our magazines, knitting and music so we could sit through the long wait. We had come prepared because we knew the days ahead could be long.

The waiting room at the clinic was filled wall to wall with people. The room was sectioned off into two rooms, people entered to one side of the room for one group of doctors, and to the other side of the room for a second group of doctors. The place was enormous, and it was still packed wall to wall with patients. The nurses come to a wall-mounted speakerphone and call the patient's name when it is time for their appointment. At promptly 10:00 they called Matt's name. We were amazed. It was the first time in years we had been to the doctor's office and the doctor was on time. We were already feeling like there was something special about this place.

A man walked us back to the doctor's office and had us take a chair. They had Matt put on a gown and sit on the examination table. It was only a short wait before the doctor came in. He greeted us, and then spent several minutes examining Matt's records. He began asking Matt several questions about how he was feeling now, how this had all began and what his initial symptoms had been. He did a very thorough job of questioning Matt and gathering a history, and then excused himself saying his associate would soon join us. When he returned he was with another doctor who began asking Matt many of the same questions. The physicians were very thorough and did not leave out anything. They wanted to know everything about Matt's diet, his medications, his sleep habits, his symptoms and his treatment.

After talking for fifteen or twenty minutes the doctor began examining Matt. He looked into his pupils, had him lift his arms overhead, and had him move his arms and legs. He had Matt push against him with his arms and briefly with his legs. The doctor asked Matt about the boots and all of the hand and wrist braces he had on. As he talked the doctor took a metal instrument and ran it along Matt's feet asking if he could feel when it was hot and when it was cold. After examining Matt for some time he asked Matt what the pain was like when he did walk. After Matt described the pain in his hips and feet the doctor had him complete another series of movements as he tested Matt's strength in his arms, legs and hips. He checked Matt for flexibility and tested the reflexes in his arms and legs. Once the doctor was done examining Matt he discussed some things he would like to do further with Matt.

One exam that he wanted to do was a test that would run electrical impulses through Matt's legs into his nerves to see how well the nerves had healed and how much conductivity there was in the legs. He also wanted Matt to have some more blood work, and to see a doctor whose specialty was rehabilitation therapy.

The doctor then asked who had been doing Matt's therapy with him, and told us we were fortunate, because whoever was doing it had made sure that Matt had maintained his strength and flexibility. The doctor was very impressed with the work Kim had done with Matt and said we were very lucky to have such a competent physical therapist. He also asked about the neurological work up that had been conducted stating they just do not see them done that thoroughly at other hospitals. He then recognized the name of our doctors and said we were fortunate to have gotten such good care. We were realizing how lucky we were that Matt had received the care he had. I was feeling good that Janet had been so persistent to make sure Matt had gotten the best of everything. Her efforts were, without question, paying off.

The next step for us at the clinic was to set up appointments for the blood work, the neurological tests, and the rehabilitation doctor. While the blood work was easy to schedule, the other two appointments could either be set for the middle of next week on consecutive days, or we had the option of trying to go on a call wait list. The call wait meant you could come early to check in, then if the clinic had a cancellation or got ahead of schedule, they would try to move Matt into an open slot. We decided to schedule appointments for the following week, but also thought we would try the call wait list tomorrow, since we had nothing else to do between appointments anyway.

We showed up at the clinic the next day bright and early. We had Matt's blood work done right away, then went and checked in to have the neurological test done. They told us they were booked solid, but if something changed they might be able to slip us in. Janet was very persistent and insisted that we needed to get in today. While she crocheted in the waiting room, Matt slept and I went to the medical library to find articles on neuropathies and related diseases. I was somewhat comforted to find an excellent article on a surgeon who had contracted a disease much similar to Matt's in 1994, and had fully recovered. The thing that struck me about the article was the description he gave of being in severe pain, and being more or less locked away in his house until he was able to work through the pain and return to work doing his own rehab therapy. He described working with a tennis ball, then weights, as he went finger by finger, toe by toe, until he was able to get back to near normal function. As I thought about Matt's long struggle he too had started with a small rubber band, then some stretching, then on to the weights. The physician in the article, like Matt, had first noticed his symptoms while driving. He too could not feel the brake and gas pedals as he was going to work. His symptoms came following a brief bout of the flu, and persisted for several months. He described the agony and loneliness of the disease, and the obstacles he ran into trying to find anyone who could treat his symptoms. His case and that of Todd McColloch of the 76's, were the only two we had found that even closely resembled Matt's. I was anxious to get back and share the article with Janet and Matt.

When I got back to waiting room Matt was gone. They had squeezed him in for the test, so we were one step closer to not having to come back next week. The nurse told Janet the test would take about an hour if we wanted to go get something to eat. Both of us agreed to wait, Matt would be hungry since he had not been able to eat after 10:00 last night for the blood work. We waited nearly an hour and a half for Matt and were becoming quite nervous. When he did emerge from the office he was pale and very sickly looking.

He had obviously been sweating and was as shaky as we had seen him in some time. When we asked him how it had gone he was rather upset with us. He said he hurt horribly, and argued if he had known they were going to do all of this to him again, he would not have come. He said they put electrodes on him, strapped him to a table, and then had him stand up. He said they then ran electric shocks through his feet and legs. Matt said he had to stand for nearly a half an hour. He said he passed out from the pain and standing up for so long. It had been months since Matt had been up for more than a few minutes. His legs and feet were shaking from the pain, and he looked miserable. He said he was just getting sick and tired of this, and wished the pain could go away and he could go home.

While we had been waiting for Matt to get done with his test, Janet had gone to the rehabilitation doctor's office and put Matt's name on the call wait list. They knew they would not have anything until late afternoon, but said we could come back after lunch and give it a try. We went to eat, and then walked around the clinic and through the downtown mall in Rochester. We wanted to buy Matt something for his big trip to the Mayo clinic, but he did not really want anything. Matt has always been a rather low maintenance child, but through this whole ordeal he had not really wanted anything. We were almost begging him to let us buy him something, but he never really wanted anything. His big thing was that when he walked again, he wanted to get the best most expensive shoes we could find. He wanted to get the best shoes made so he could take real good care of his feet.

At precisely 1:00 we went back to the waiting room. We had found the clinic is very good about being on time, so we did not want to be late for any appointments. We were a little discouraged because about 500 other people were there too. People were putting together jig-saw puzzles, reading books and generally looking like they had waited for some time. As we looked for a place to sit Matt spotted a lady knitting a sweater across the room. He bet me that Janet would go over and talk to that lady once we sat down. No sooner had we found a chair than Janet was off like a shot to see what the gal was making. When Matt and I both started laughing she knew something was up. I think we had all just been together way too long, but it was fun seeing Matt relaxing a bit. This was the first time I had seen him laugh and joke in some time. He was apparently feeling good about being at the clinic.

We waited for an hour or two to get an appointment but had no luck. Finally Janet went up the front desk and explained our situation. While she thought it would help, I told her that everyone in the room had probably traveled for hours and that the nurses had probably heard stories such as ours a thousand times a day. Nonetheless, Janet tried to plead her case to get Matt in despite my doubts that it would work. She was becoming more and more persistent the more we dealt with all of these medical people. The nurse told Janet that we could come back around 3:30; they might be able to squeeze Matt in sometime after that. With that said, we were off like a shot to our neurologist's office to see if we could get an appointment with him. If we got in to the rehabilitation doctor this afternoon, then were able to get Matt back in to see the neurologist tomorrow, we could possibly get this whole trip done in three days, and not have to make a return trip. Janet was doing some extremely fast talking to make all of this happen. The neuro's desk was willing, but said they did not know if they would be able to get all of the other tests back in time to do any good for that appointment. Janet went around to each of the offices one more time to ensure that all of right reports etc. would be sent, and that we were set for the next day. We were optimistic we might actually get this trip done in one short week.

 The rehabilitation doctor's appointment was just like the others we had had. At 3:30 promptly they called Matt's name. We met with an intern initially who took a very thorough history from Matt. In all of our appointments we were impressed with how long the doctors spent with Matt. Once again, they were very thorough. This doctor too had known Matt's initial neurologist from home and also asked about the physical therapist that had been working with Matt. As he examined Matt, he was very impressed with his strength and the way they had worked his hip and calf muscles to keep him ready for when he walked. The intern left for a short time, then returned with the rehabilitation doctor. This doctor was a little more physical with Matt and pushed and prodded him and tried to find the spots that really hurt. He talked with Matt about the pain in his feet, and tried to touch Matt's feet. He too asked who had been doing physical therapy with Matt, and was very impressed. They were totally amazed at how well they had worked Matt's legs and upper body despite the damaged nerves. It had been like putting together the pieces of a jigsaw puzzle, and apparently Kim had done a very good job with Matt. The doctor could not believe how thorough they had been in not letting Matt's other muscles deteriorate. This doctor did feel the epidural block would have been a waste of time for Matt since it would have deadened all of the nerves, not just the ones we needed. He felt we had made the right decision holding off on it, and advised we not do it at this time. He said it appeared Matt's recovery was going very well, but a little slow. He advised that, unless the blood work would show something else, the key at this point might be working harder and having Matt work more to push through the pain. He said he was going to recommend some changes in the medication to help Matt with the pain, but said at this point a lot of the recovery was up to Matt and how much pain he could tolerate. While it would not be easy, he was optimistic Matt would recover and get back to normal. These were some of the best words we had heard in months!

As we were leaving I pushed Matt out in his wheelchair. Janet went back to ask the doctor if there was more Kim could be doing with Matt in therapy or if there was anything more we could do with water therapy, etc. He too told Janet everything Kim was doing was perfect; now Matt just needed to keep motivated and push through the pain. While we had heard this all before, the reality that Matt was going to get better and that it was up to him at this point was refreshing. The only thing I kept thinking back to the article I had read in the Mayo library about the doctor with this disease. He talked about how hard it was for people to understand, and how painful and lonely this was. He said people could not imagine or understand the pain of the disease, and that that was one of the hardest parts of the whole process; pushing through pain you could barely tolerate. The news for us meant that we were doing everything that needed to be done, this was just the reinforcement we needed at this point.

We went back to the motel that evening hopeful we would be able to have one last appointment the next day and be on our way. When we got to the room our cell phone rang and there was a message from Josh. Today was the day that seniors picked up caps and gowns. He wanted to be sure Matt's got picked up, and wondered if he should get it for us. That was the crazy thing about all of this for us. In the middle of all the pain, the therapy and the trying to get better, in the middle of all of that, the world just never slowed down. Things like caps and gowns and graduation seemed so unimportant and so distant, but at the same time, we had this sense that if we did not try to keep up, Matt would just get further and further behind until there was no chance of Matt catching up. We were lucky people like Josh were thinking ahead, because much of the time, we were just living day to day.

The next day we were up again bright and early and off to the clinic. We packed our van and checked out of the motel room before we boarded the shuttle. Janet was feeling pretty smug about herself knowing she had been able to pull off all of the appointments in such a short time. We were extremely lucky that we did not have to come back several more times and that the scheduling worked out like it did. What could have involved several more trips back to Mayo, and months to schedule, was all being accomplished in just over a three-day time span. We were very fortunate.

We arrived at the clinic well ahead of time once again, but knew by now that when it was time for our appointment, the doctors would be right on time. At precisely 9:00 they once again called Matt's name. We were a little anxious about what all of the tests had shown. What if the blood tests had found something else? What if the neurological tests found more damage than we realized? Our minds were racing with fear. As we sat down and waited for the doctor, Matt sat head slumped and dozed off into a deep sleep. He looked very worn. He had put in some long days at the clinic and was not used to being up so much. The days were beginning to take their toll on him and it showed. While we knew he needed to begin pushing himself more physically, the balance was not pushing so much that he went backwards. Today he looked like he was balancing on a thin line and he looked very rough. He was also probably as worried as we were about what they would find. When the doctor came in Matt continued to sit slumped over. He showed very little interest in what the doctor was saying, and he appeared to be preparing himself for the worst. As the doctor began talking he started by saying everything was very positive. They had found nothing new. The nerves were all pretty well healed, the muscles were well toned and strong and the blood work all looked normal. They were feeling positive that Matt would make a full recovery. How long recovery would take was up to Matt and how much he could push himself and how much pain he could tolerate. They were positive our therapy was helping and his progress was continuing; albeit slow, it <u>was</u> progressing. The doctor saw no reason to follow up with him further at the clinic. He believed Matt should continue physical therapy. It was definitely working and we were fortunate to have someone as excellent as Kim taking care of Matt. They felt Kim had brought Matt along wonderfully. The doctors were going to change the dosages of his medications; upping the Neurotin and slowly taking Matt off the Baclofen. The thought was that more Neurotin would help deal with the pain even more, while the Baclofen might actually be making Matt's muscles tighter and weaker. The report was extremely positive! Matt would heal at the rate that he was able to tolerate doing more, but he would heal! They still were not able to make a conclusive diagnosis, but the result of whatever Matt had was Peripheral Neuropathy that had affected the nerves of his legs and feet. We actually knew little more than before, but we did know Matt was getting better.

Graduating With Honor(s)

I think we were all pretty exhausted on the ride home. We had talked with Janet's brother Ron about visiting them in Austin a short way from Rochester on our way home. If we had enough time we could see the Spam Museum and maybe tour the Hormel plant that Ron works at as we went through. Janet called and left a message for Ron as we left Rochester, and said we would stop by on our way through if we heard back from them. Ron called nearly three hours later. Janet and Matt had fallen asleep right outside of Rochester and woke only when the phone rang. They had slept for over three hours, and would have probably slept longer if the cell phone had not rung. As they woke I was again reminded how wearing this really was on all of us.

CHAPTER 18
PANCAKES ANYONE?

After returning from Mayo it was kind of a bittersweet time. We really did not know anything more, except that Matt was to increase the dosage of one medication and be weaned off of the other. The visit to Mayo did seem to improve Matt's motivation and he began stepping up his workouts a bit. He was now going to the pool a couple of times a week, was working with Kim a couple of times a week and was beginning try to ride the stationary bike at home. This prompted me to get a new exercise bike in our basement. Matt and I soon began having contests to see who could ride the farthest at a certain level for a designated length of time. It amazed me that despite the way he wobbled and shook when he tried to walk, that he was able to climb on the exercise bide and ride me within an inch or two of my life. While I was no Lance Armstrong, I am a runner and was in the process of training for a marathon. I just could not believe with all of the miles I was running, and as sick as he was that he could ride right with me. Either I was older than I thought, or he was better than we thought. Either way we were having some interesting biking competitions in our basement several times a week. Matt began pushing himself more, and more, and it was obvious that he needed the advice from the doctors at

Mayo and he was now more determined than ever to have his illness to end, and end soon.

After returning from the Mayo Clinic we had one more setback. I had a bout with kidney stones that put me in the hospital and required surgery. I spent nearly two weeks with a catheter in and taking pain pills. Poor Janet was left doing everything during this time. As the next couple of weeks passed we were feeling very run down and stressed.

With everything that was going on it felt like the benefit to be held for Matt came out of nowhere. The benefit was to be at the grade school attached to our church. The flyers for the banquet were all over town, radio stations were announcing the benefit and everyone we talked to was planning to come. We were still quite overwhelmed by the whole idea, and tried to be as calm and collected as we could be about the whole thing for Matt's sake. We were figuring that it would be a fairly big affair, but we did not want to let on to him that it would be anything but a few friends. He was already not handling the attention very well, and he was growing very tired of this image of himself as being a sick kid. The last thing in the world he wanted was for people to feel sorry for him.

Despite feeling miserable from my kidney stone and the resulting complications, I ran ten miles that Saturday to try to begin preparing for an upcoming marathon. At times I thought I was completely crazy trying to run in the middle of all of this, but I had run the Lincoln Marathon 23 years in a row, and did not want to break my streak now.

Besides, maybe a year from now Matt would be well enough to run with me again, who knows?

The day of the benefit arrived and we were all up very early. Ann was going to say a prayer to open the benefit, so we rushed to be there by 8:00 so we could partake in that prayer. Unfortunately, like so many times that Matt was rushed, things just did not go well. This morning was not any better. His legs were hurting and began shaking. His stomach became upset and he began to get a headache. At 8:15 he looked up the stairs and said he did not think he could go. By now his legs were in fairly constant spasms. Neither Janet nor I were going to accept no for an answer this morning and no matter how much pain he was in, or how bad he was shaking, he was going. This was the second time I remember grabbing the bottle of Oxycotin. I gave him one along with the rest of his medications, and prayed it did not wipe him out so bad he was a zombie all day.

We neared the school around 8:30 expecting to be able to find a parking spot right by the gym since the first mass would not get out for another half an hour. As we neared the parking lot Janet and I looked at each other and just went WOW! The parking lot was already full and the first church service had not even gotten over yet. We managed to find a place to park, then began to unload Matt. By now Matt was beginning to realize how many people were already there, and he began getting nervous. He blamed us for not telling him there would be this many people and he began panicking. He was worried that he would not know what to say, and that he would not know many of the people.

He said he did not want to be a spectacle, and was worried about how he looked. He said he just did not want this kind of attention. He wanted to be walking again before people saw him. He just hated being like this today and it showed more than ever.

As Matt continued growing more panicky Janet became <u>very</u> deliberate with him by explaining that today he had to be strong. He had to be at the benefit to thank all of the people who had worked so hard to put it on for him. This was his opportunity to show them he was appreciative and deserving of their prayers and gifts. He had to learn how to except people's gifts, and today was going to be a good place to start. Though Matt was very unsure of himself initially, he seemed to relax once he realized people were there to support him, not to look at him. Although he was very uncomfortable with how he looked and the fact that he was in a wheelchair, he realized people cared, and because of that he had to be accepting of their kindness. Matt began to make the decision that day that he had to accept the fact that bad things had happened to him, and there was nothing he could do about it. He had to accept that he was now different and that that was not necessarily bad. It just meant he was different. While this was a hard lesson for him to learn, the morning of the benefit he seemed to come to grips more with what had happened to him.

We entered the benefit around 8:30 am. Ann had already said her prayer and we were very disappointed we had missed it. It was funny, but there were just some things that we felt like we needed going through all of this, and a little as it seems, that prayer was something we grieved about missing for some time. Several times since that day, both Janet and I have talked about not being there to pray that morning with our closest friends. It was just something that was very important to us, and we were very sad we missed it. The gym was already full of people when we got there. The benefit was to be held from 8:00 AM to 1:00 PM but we had no idea what to expect. The overwhelming response from the start was an indication of what the day would bring.

From the time we entered the school gym to the time the benefit ended we were just in total awe. Everywhere we turned there were friends, neighbors and acquaintances that had showed up to support Matt. People we had not seen for years and people we see everyday stood in line to eat pancakes and offer their support for Matt. As we watched Matt that day we began to realize that he was far more courageous than we ever realized. He had battled constantly since last October fighting off the physical and emotional pain of having everything in his life change. A year ago his goal was to work hard his senior year and graduate with honors. Today he was sitting here struggling as best he could to maintain his dignity and honor. And thank God, with him still were his friends Jason, Josh, Emily, Sarah, David, Luke and Danny, helping him to have the courage to carry on one more day.

As we watched the people at the benefit come and go we were overwhelmed with emotion. We could not believe the love and support being shown for our son, yet we struggled still with the bitterness of having this happen to him. It seemed as though everyone we knew was there. People from our Kids' soccer teams, school classmates, teachers, coaches, friends neighbors, and people from the church, and last but not least, Smitty and the O'Gorman Jazz band. Matt loved every minute of the benefit and though it got his legs hurting and he was pumping pain pills by the dozen the smile of appreciation on his face was one of sheer delight.

While there were dozens of highlights from the day, one that particularly stuck with me was one time mid-morning when I saw Matt wheeling full speed for the door. He had a big smile on his face and was pushing very quickly looking anxious and excited. Andrea Wilson, the O'Gorman gymnast who had fallen and ended up in a wheelchair had been in Denver undergoing rehab. She had just gotten back in town a few days ago and had shown up for the benefit. Her presence had obviously helped to make Matt's day. While I would be surprised if he had said more than three words to her the whole time she was there, it was important to him to see that she was o.k. and that she was getting better. He was very concerned for her, and tried following her progress very closely. He would often talk about how strong she was and how he did not know if he could go through what she had. It was ironic, because so many of us were thinking the same thing about him. To him she was a hero; to us, he was a hero.

As the benefit began winding down Janet came up to me upset because she was not getting to thank everyone. She felt bad because people were coming and going before she got a chance to thank everyone. She was amazed at the people who were there, and the amount of work they had gone through for Matt. From our Knights of Columbus members who served over 1200 plates of pancakes, to our friends who helped cook the sausage, for hours on end we were beside ourselves for words to say to all of the people who had supported the event.

The benefit had been a success. It had raised thousands of dollars for Matt's expenses, and we counted nearly 1000 people who were in attendance. While we had not emphasized the money, between the medical bills and the time Janet had taken off, money was becoming lean. If nothing else, the money would guarantee that we would have some funds set aside to send Matt to college this fall, if that was still an option. But more importantly, the benefit taught Matt an important lesson. That lesson was that the effort he was putting forth to beat this illness was not going unnoticed. People were amazed at his strength, at his courage, at his willingness to continue to fight back. He had surely gained the respect of the community. Even after this epitome of a day all this young man only wanted was to return home, crawl into the basement and go to sleep. Courage takes a lot of energy!

CHAPTER 19
SETTING GOALS

The benefit was one more shot in the arm Matt needed. It seemed at each time during the year that Matt was down and at his worst someone else found a way to push him forward. Early on Josh had carried him, during the cold winter months the visits from the pep band had carried him, when he began getting discouraged an article about he and Andrea in the school newspaper helped to carry him and to refocus his energy toward getting well. These and hundreds of other both small and large pieces of support seemed to keep him going. The benefit, though, seemed to make Matt realize that no matter what; he had caught the eye of the community. He seemed to be thinking now that if everyone was watching, he had better at least give this his best try. At times he even admitted he felt like he was now under more pressure to get better. He felt like he owed it to everybody. Following the benefit Matt began setting new goals and working hard to reach them.

The first goal Matt set was that he would begin to walk by Easter. He knew that most of Janet's family would be back for the holiday, and he wanted to be a lot better by then. Matt began working harder in therapy, and was riding the exercise bike more than ever. He was now trying to use his walker more, and tried to get up more and more around the house. While his heart was in it, Matt continued to compare the pain to walking on sharp needles or razor blades. At its best it felt like electric shocks running up and down his legs. At its worst, the pain was like a razor blade cutting into the foot. The problem was that he knew the cut was coming and he had to step anyway. This was the hardest part for him, knowing it was going to hurt, and knowing it was that hurt he had to overcome to get better.

As Easter rolled around Matt was getting better and better at standing. He could get up for longer periods of time, and was now beginning to take a few small steps. Kim had held him off from trying to walk until now because he did not want him trying to walk on his toes and feet when they kept curling under. They had worked on desensitizing the feet until they had reached the point that Matt could now touch his feet down for a few seconds. He was now able to put slippers on as long as they did not touch his heels, and he was coming closer to being able to bear all of his weight on his feet. The progress continued to be slow, but it was progress. His goal, the first goal we had heard from him, was to walk at Easter.

Janet's relatives began arriving early for Easter and came over to see Matt one by one. It was hard on him because most still could not understand what he was dealing with, and could not understand why he could not walk. His oldest cousin Mike offered to go to therapy with Matt to help him. Matt had usually been pretty private about letting people see him work out, but he did agree to let Mike come. The two of them went to therapy and lifted weights together then went through Matt's normal routine of stretching, standing and isometrics. Then, for the first time since his early stay in the hospital, Matt stood up with his walker and did some real walking. He went around the room leaving the protection of the parallel bars and just pushed the walker by himself. This was the first sign we had seen that Matt really was returning to normal. For the first time in months, he was able to walk a few steps.

The Saturday before Easter Matt had a pretty tough day. The workout and walking had taken a lot out of him, and he was complaining that his legs were burning and more painful than they had been in some time. We had now made the changes to his medications as they had recommended at the Mayo Clinic. The changes left Matt completely wiped out and tired all of the time. It was getting to the point that he would spend most of the day sleeping, work out a few hours, then lay down again. While he was still progressing, it was very slow. He was getting so frustrated with not being able to do what he wanted, when he wanted. On days like these, it took all of the patience he had not to get totally frustrated and just give up.

When we went to the motel to join his cousins for the Easter meal Matt was very tired and groggy and was not feeling very well. When he tried to transfer himself from his wheelchair to a room chair his wheelchair slipped and tipped over. He fell under the wheelchair and just lay there in shock and frustration. This was the first time Matt had really fallen, and he was just about at the end of his rope. When was enough going to be enough? His brothers immediately came to get me, and he was still just laying with a kind of dazed look on his face, when I finally got to him. He had scraped up his face a little and was obviously feeling rather embarrassed. Once we got Matt back into his chair and into a more private area he complained that he just felt so out of it. He was groggy, could not get any energy and said he hurt all over. He complained that he was just having too many of these days. Both he and the rest of us were hoping this would all just end, but the reality was it just kept going on and on.

On Easter Sunday Matt got up and made the effort to go to church and attend the normal Easter with everyone else. He was in a better mood, but still seemed quite groggy and in a daze. It was at times like this that it was hard to know how much he should push himself, and how much he should just rest. The harder he pushed himself some days, the less he seemed to accomplish. Yet the doctors kept telling him to push himself and to do more. Our frustration was the doctors never really saw him enough to know what he was really going through. While he seemed to understand his limits it was tough to watch him on days like these when he was obviously suffering, and there was nothing we could do.

After eating our Easter meal and conducting the annual Easter Egg hunt Matt announced it was now time for him to walk. While we had not pushed him about his goal of walking today, he obviously had it in his mind that he was committed to walking. He asked his cousin Mike to help so Janet and I stood by and watched. Matt stood by his walker and slowly took one step, then two, then three, and then four. He walked several yards before his feet and legs were shaking so hard he could no longer stand. What a site! Matt clinging to his walker; cousin

Mike pulling him along, and Janet and I pushing the wheelchair from behind in case he fell. While it was not the most impressive walk and it was not the farthest walk, it was Matt's first attempt at walking, and it had gone well. Not the prettiest or most successful walk, but a walk just the same.

After his big walk at Easter Matt began to have more and more bad days. The school called me one morning the next week to say they had Matt in the teachers' lounge. He had become dizzy in class and they were worried he would fall out of his wheelchair. When I went to pick him up at school he was sitting in the teachers lounge with two of the faculty. He was sound asleep and dead to the world. Drool was running down his cheeks and when I woke him his eyes were all red and blood shot because he had been sleeping so soundly. I apologized to the teachers and thanked them for looking after Matt. I explained that they had increased his medications considerably, and that we were still trying to get them adjusted. I laughed that obviously we still had a ways to go. As I was pushing Matt out of the lounge, I thought the school probably thought we were great parents sending our kid to school so medicated he could not even stay awake. Matt went home that afternoon and slept the rest of the afternoon and evening. The next day we called the doctor and she agreed it was time to begin cutting down on his medications. The benefit of the pain control was outweighed by Matt's inability to function. It was such a balancing act; between keeping his pain under control and keeping him alert and motivated enough to keep going.

As we began to decrease Matt's medications we were hoping it would help so that he could make it through the next few weeks. We were now into late April and graduation was set to happen within the next couple of weeks. It was going to be a busy time for Matt, and if he was to salvage anything from his senior year he was going to have to do it within the next few weeks. We were decreasing his meds on a daily basis hoping he would come around. When he complained about the pain or burning we would give him an Advil or Aleve and hope that would take care of his pain for a while. We were well aware that the heavily medicated route was not working, and that he would need to tolerate the pain a little more in the weeks ahead.

Kim was continuing to push Matt in therapy during this time. He was doing more and more biking to strengthen his hips and thighs, and he had Matt begin to use half crutches with braces to begin to walk. Matt took to these crutches quickly seeing them as the next step to real walking. Matt hadn't had these crutches for even a week yet when he announced his next goal! HE WOULD WALK AT GRADUATION! While Janet and I had talked about what he would do at graduation, it had not been something we had really wanted to talk about with him. We knew the idea of receiving his diploma in a wheelchair would not appeal to him, but we did not really have any idea about what else he could do. While we were a little skeptical, this was only the second goal Matt had set for himself, and for now his plan was that he <u>was </u>going to walk across the stage at graduation. More than ever it was what he wanted to happen next.

CHAPTER 20
GRADUATION NEARS

The next week started with the National Honor Society Convocation held early in the week at the high school. It is a nice celebration by Matt's high school for students who had worked hard and achieved academic success. Many students such as Matt who had been inducted into the National Honor Society last year were seated across from the students being inducted this year. This ceremony was one of the reminders for us about how the year had really gone. Last year Matt was a National Honor Society inductee who was among the leaders in his class. He pushed himself academically and in extracurricular activities and was pushing to become one of the top students in his class. As we watched him being pushed in his wheel chair to the front of the group, it was a reminder to us of how difficult this year had been. Not only had Matt not been able to reach his goals academically and in his extracurricular activities, but also it was obvious that he was hanging on at this point just to make it through the year. As physically beat up as he had been, studying and being a leader was the last thing he had on his mind. Matt was doing all he could just to make it through the day.

The next big day leading to graduation was the seniors honors day. It was a ceremony that honored students for their accomplishments and provided an opportunity for the school to recognize the senior class for its accomplishments. The event honored students for the awards they had received and for the scholarships they have been offered. As Janet and I watched the ceremony we were awestruck at the accomplishments of many of Matt's classmates. All state band, all state choir, presidential scholars, and as a class, millions of dollars in scholarship offers. The list went on and on. Several students were recognized for the scholarships they had received including prestigious scholarships to schools such as MIT and Notre Dame. One student had received over $700,000 in scholarship offers, while many in the class had received over $100,000 in offers. As we watched the ceremony and many of Matt's friends being recognized, we could not help but wonder how the year would have been different if Matt had not gotten so ill and struggled so much just to hang on. While it was painful to think of what might have been, it was even more painful to think of what was yet to come. Matt still had a very long road ahead of him.

Matt had worked very hard academically his entire life. He had received good grades, and was still nearly a 4.0 student. But the reality was he was concentrating so much on just getting through the year that it was doubtful there would much, if anything, in scholarships for him. All of this was a bittersweet ending. Matt had worked so hard for so many years, yet the tragedy of the past year was going to be with him for some time. This realization came upon us as graduation neared.

As we watched the ceremony, the pain of knowing what might have been and what should have been was overwhelming. We were beginning to grieve for all we had lost. As I watched Matt in the middle of this ceremony, I could not help but wonder how he was handling this. To know what could have been, his heart must have been breaking. His plans for being one of the top students were now relegated to being lucky to be a student at all. Watching him the feelings about the injustice of all of this was overwhelming.

After leaving the senior awards ceremony it seemed like the swirl of emotions just kept getting bigger. Janet had received a call a few weeks prior asking if we would speak at the joint school board meeting for the local Catholic Schools. They wanted to hear about our experiences during this past year with Matt in the schools. The high school principal had asked us to visit with the board and the administration to provide them some insight in regard to what our year had been like. He felt we would have some interesting insight for the board to hear. While Janet and I were not certain what we would talk about, we knew we wanted to use the time to thank the faculty and administration for all that they had done for Matt. One of the issues the schools were struggling with was the lack of handicapped accessibility at the high school. The problems Matt had had when he returned to school had been a major issue. He was unable to go to the bathroom because they did not have a accessible restroom that would accommodate his wheel chair. He was not able to eat lunch because the lunchroom was down a flight a stairs. Even taking certain classes was a problem because it meant either going down stairs, or going outside around the entire building in his wheelchair. In the winter and on rainy days this was just not doable because his clothes, books and papers ended up soaked. While Matt had been upset with all of the fuss he was creating for the school, when Andrea fell and also became wheelchair bound he was glad that he had come first and partially paved the way. Since they had to deal with his wheelchair they were a little better prepared for her. His struggle this year had not been without some benefit.

As Janet and I wrestled with what we would say to school board, we agreed we would need to write it down so we would not just ramble all over the place. We also agreed that since Janet had been very emotional in talking about Matt, I would get up and read our comments. I was very adamant that we would use this time to thank everyone for their help this year and to write down our comments so we would not leave anyone out. As I drove to the meeting I had the notes in my pocket and was feeling pretty good about what I was going to say. I was happy we were going to get this opportunity to thank everyone, and was feeling glad that some of the people that had gone out of their way to help Matt would be recognized for their efforts.

Janet and I met at the meeting and sat at a table that included Smitty, the band instructor, and a couple of staff who were to be recognized for their contributions to the district. As the meeting went on they thanked several people for their work throughout the year, and they discussed the good year the Catholic Schools had been fortunate enough to have. As the meeting progressed there were several of our friends who spoke and who were in attendance at the meeting. As the time for us to talk neared, I could begin to feel myself swelling up with emotion. I was so touched by the fact that we were sitting in the middle of a group of people who had really made a difference in our son's life this past year.

As the superintendent of the Catholic Schools introduced Janet and I, we calmly went to the microphone and I pulled our pre written notes from my pocket. I calmly approached the microphone and as I began to speak, a year's worth of emotion began pouring out. All of the things I wanted to say were all of a sudden becoming very difficult to say. As I began sobbing, I quickly realized I was not going to be able to compose myself long enough to get through even the first sentence. I quickly handed the notes to Janet and she attempted to read the words on the paper. She read for a brief time, then she too broke into tears. I took the notes from her and was able to read only a couple of more sentences before I broke down again. And so it went, until we progressed through our notes, sentence by sentence, first me, then Janet, then me. We took turns thanking all of the people who had helped Matt and our entire family get through the year. From the classmates and teachers who had visited Matt to the Administrators and staff who had looked after Chris and Andrew as they had struggled through the year. We thanked everyone; Andrew's teachers and classmates for their daily prayers, Chris's principal, "Ms. B." for taking the time to ask Chris daily about Matt, to Matt's instructors who had mentioned Matt daily in their Mass Intentions. These were little things, but things that one by one, card by card, prayer by prayer, call by call, had added up to an enormous amount of support for an isolated young man spending his year in a basement bound to a wheelchair. By the time Janet and I finished there was not a dry eye in the house. Everyone thanked us for sharing our journey with them, and we thanked them for having taken this journey with us.

When I got home that evening I was emotionally drained. Janet was also wiped out and both of us were feeling bad that we had not gotten to thank everyone that we wanted to during our presentation to the school board. While we had hoped to thank more people, the emotion of the day had just been too much for us to deal with. As we sat there that evening the phone began to ring off the hook. Friends, neighbors, and even complete strangers that had heard us at the meeting were calling to thank us and to share with us how powerful our presentation had been for everyone. Many people were aware of the year we had had, while others called to apologize they had not been there for us. As we talked that evening, we began to realize how significant this past year really had been in our lives. As the calls continued, one we received was from a media person who had heard us talk that day. He wanted to know if we would be willing to share Matt's story with the local television station. We said we would have to think about it and talk it over with Matt.

As we discussed the issue with Matt he was still concerned that he just did not want to draw any attention to himself. He said he felt bad that people were talking about him and he felt bad that they were worrying about him when someone like Andrea could really use the attention. As we discussed it, we shared with Matt that it was up to him, but that this would be his only opportunity to thank everyone that had helped him during the past year. We told him we did not know how we could possibly thank everyone for what they had done, but that if we were going to have an opportunity to thank people like Josh and Jason it would be now. Matt thought this over and then agreed. He said he wanted the opportunity to thank everyone that had helped him during the year. I was impressed with how much he too was appreciating what everyone had done for him.

Graduation was now only a week or two away and we were continuing to feel the build up. We received a call from one of the administrators at the school asking how we wanted to set up the stage for Matt at graduation. He said that the intention was to have a hoist for Matt and Andrea that would lift them onto the stage. They would then go onto the stage, accept their diplomas, and then they would go back to the lift and be hoisted down. He said the only issue with the lift was that the boys sat at one side of the stage, and the girls at the other. He said they would need to decide where to put the lift, and that it would mean either Matt would need to sit with the girls or Andrea would need to sit with the boys. As we talked, I said I would talk to Matt. Without hesitation Matt told me he would not need a lift. His intent was to walk across the stage and accept his diploma. He said he would **not** accept his diploma in a wheelchair. When I told the principal this on the phone it was obvious he was concerned about Matt's ability to do this. He said the stairs were not very wide, and he would not want to see Matt embarrass himself or fall. I told him Matt had been walking with crutches in therapy, so that for now we wanted to see if we could make this work for him. As we talked I told him to put the lift on the girls' side of the stage. If worst came to worst Matt could sit on the girls' side of the stage. While I didn't know if Matt could walk across the stage, I knew that we had to honor him enough at this point to let him give it a try.

The next few days at therapy Matt really began working with his crutches. It became apparent that his intent was to walk across the stage and accept his diploma. He and Kim talked about it and apparently Kim was feeling rather nervous about it too. He offered to come to graduation to help Matt across the stage, but Matt said he would be fine. If he needed help he would get Josh and Jason to help him. That would only be appropriate as the two of them had carried Matt a long way this year, and if Matt needed to be helped across the stage they should be the ones to do it. Matt was determined that he would walk across the stage. If he needed crutches, it would be the same ones he had used all year, Josh and Jason. It was done. Matt had made up his mind; come hell or high water he would walk across the stage. How he would do it was not certain, but he was determined that he would walk across the stage.

CHAPTER 21
GRADUATION

Two days before graduation the media showed up to begin interviewing Matt, Janet and I. We really wanted to talk about all of the friends and family that had helped us during the past several months and to try to convey our thanks to all of the people who had helped Matt during the past year. As we talked with the reporter it was difficult to communicate exactly what had happened to Matt. People just could not connect mono with the young man they saw in the wheelchair. As we talked I pulled out all of our articles on peripheral neuropathy, Todd McCulloch of the 76ers and anything else I could find to help them to understand. The more we talked the more engrossed the reporters became in the story until they began asking the "how did you handle it all?" question. At that point Janet and I began to break down. Not once since Matt had been in the hospital and we had been told to be strong for him had we broken down in front of Matt. But now as we spoke to the reporter a whole year's worth of emotion began spilling forth. Like our speech before the school board, we tag teamed until we finally made it through the interview. At that point even the reporter had tears in his eyes. Matt's portion of the interview was much more together than our half had been. Later, when we watched it, we again sensed how much strength and determination this young man of ours really had. He had sat in this basement, on a couch hide-bed for nearly eight months patiently fighting this painful crippling disease. He had beat the pain, fought through the emotions, and been stronger than even Janet and I had realized. As we watched him in the interview, the reporters questioned him several times about how he could do this and what allowed him to go on. As they questioned Matt his answers were simple, deliberate, but honest. "I had no choice, I had to accept what was happening, and just go on." It was at that point that it dawned on me. He very much knew what was happening; he was very frightened and very afraid. But, he also knew he had no choice but to accept what was happening and go on. Then, as he answered the "how of it", we heard Matt thank the people who had helped him the most during the past year. We were fully hoping he would thank Josh and Jason, but to our surprise Matt said "I could never had made it through the past year without my mom and dad!" Matt had said it daily for months, but now he had told the world "Thanks Mom, Thanks Dad".

That night the interview ran on the local television station and our phone began ringing off the hook. Friends who knew, and friends who didn't were all reaching out to support us one more time, and all of them were praying for Matt and for his walk across the stage. During the interview, Matt had put the ultimate pressure on himself by announcing on air that his goal on graduation night was to walk across the stage. He had told the world "I will walk across the stage tomorrow night." It was what he had to do to make his graduation mean something.

Graduating With Honor(s)

The next day was graduation day. A reporter from the local newspaper came out and spent a couple of hours interviewing Matt, Janet and I. During this interview we were able to begin thanking people, but again, the story was to be, Matt's goal to walk across the stage that night. The reporter said they would have someone there to take pictures, and the television crew called to say they would be there to catch the big moment on camera. Matt had barely walked twenty steps at home or in therapy, and here he was planning to walk across the stage, in front of the media and a thousand other people.

Graduation rehearsal that afternoon was at the school and not at the actual auditorium where the graduation would be held. They had the students' line up and practiced having them march in. After the rehearsal Janet and Matt decided they wanted to go look at the stage and the steps to see how difficult the task would be that evening. They wanted to actually see the stairs to see how difficult it would be getting up them. More importantly, they wanted to see how hard it would be coming down. At this point Matt had not even attempted to try going down any stairs with his crutches, but this night would be the night. When they arrived at the auditorium to check the place out they were not alone; Josh, Jason, Dave and a group of others had also come. It was obvious; Matt was not going to make this walk alone.

As the time for graduation neared the pressure was enormous. All of the emotions of the last year were building one more time and I knew this was going to be a tough evening for everyone. As we pulled up to the auditorium the parking lot was already full. They had one section fenced off and Janet told me to go in there it was the only handicapped parking in the lot, and even if it meant going around the fence we were going to use it. Once we got through the fence there was one other car there; Andrea's. It was emotional just knowing the two in wheelchairs were already joined before they even entered the building.

Once we got into the building the press was already there. Fortunately, they saw Matt, but left him alone. They did start interviewing his friends, but at that point we were all so nervous I don't think any of us could have talked anyway. Janet and I took Matt back to be with his class, then scrambled to find chairs. When the school people saw us, they helped us to find chairs right at the back of the class. By now the people around us were joking that they were getting to sit next to the celebrities. We were slowly beginning to feel like celebrities, though we really did wish it had been under different circumstances.

As the students marched in Janet and I were beginning to feel the tension build. We were very anxious and it was beginning to show. My mom had come down for the graduation and asked me what would happen if Matt was not able to get up the stairs and fell. She said he was not looking that strong today, and she was worried he would not be able to make it. I told her that at this point it did not matter. If Matt fell he would just crawl across the stage. He was going to make it and that was all there was to it!

Once the class sat down the irony of life continued. Sitting right in front of us was Josh. His face was beet red, he was sweating, and he was coughing uncontrollably. The conference track meet had been

Graduating With Honor(s)

that day, and he had literally just walked off the track from running the two-mile, and had come to graduation. It was obvious he was not feeling well. As the graduation progressed, other students walked in during graduation. They had run races that had actually made them late for their own gradation. As I looked around the class, I could not see Matt. He was near the front of the crowd, and as the class stood he was difficult to see in his wheelchair. Andrea was sitting right across the aisle from us, and her boyfriend also named Matt, kept snapping pictures of her and getting her to look over at him smiling. It was a nice distraction from all of the tension as he kept her and the classmates around him laughing and at ease. Those two young people had been through the most difficult of years' imaginable!

As the speeches began I became more and more nervous. Josh was sweating and as the heat in the building rose, I was beginning to have my doubts that Josh would make it through graduation; let alone Matt. As the speakers progressed, and the actual ceremony neared, Janet and I became more and more nervous. Chris and Andrew began teasing me because I looked so tense, and it was obvious this was going to be an anxious time for all of us. I began crossing my fingers, just hoping for the best.

I concentrated hard to listen to the speeches by the student class representatives. Kelly Mutchler had been over to see Matt several times and had written an article in the school newspaper about Matt. I listened very intently to her speech, admiring her intellect and wit. When she concluded, the next speaker was to be the Bishop. He stood

Daniel D. Deal

up and made a few remarks, then turned the program over to the priest from the high school.

As I sat back to listen, I realized rather quickly, that the topic of his graduation speech was to be Matt and Andrea. He talked about triumphs, and struggles, and how sometimes we start life and one point and end up at a different point. He stood by Matt and asked if this is where Matt Deal had expected he would be at the end of this senior year; in a wheelchair ready to graduate? Then he went to Andrea and asked if this state champion gymnast ever expected she would be where she was? He talked about the twists and turns life takes, and how we need to be strong and persevere; just like Matt and Andrea had. By now my heart was firmly in my throat. In addition to the emotion of having Matt walk across the stage, the entire graduation was now focused on he and Andrea. They had obviously caught the attention of the school and by now of the audience and a large part of our community. As I looked around the room I could see the lines of cameras everywhere; the reporter from the newspaper, and there, in the stands pointing the direction of Matt, was the cameraman from the local television station. By now we had come to refer to him as Budda. As he filmed I began to appreciate what he too was doing for Matt. The way he handled the story, and the manner in which he talked to Matt. He seemed so impressed by the drive and motivation Matt had. Little did he know, he too, was one of the people that were helping to push Matt to the next step. As the media coverage grew, so did Matt's determination not to let anyone down.

Graduating With Honor(s)

As the priest continued his speech I began to clamp down on my lip and try to hold on. I could feel the tears coming, but was trying to do my best to hold them back. I could no longer look at Janet knowing the tears would flow if I did. She was busying herself with the camera making sure she got some photos of the event. Chris and Andrew were sitting back being cool, but they too were no doubt feeling pretty emotional. Andrew began tugging on my suit coat, teasing me that I was beginning to cry. Chris sat slouched back looking through his long bangs just trying to be cool. As we sat there we were aware that nearly every eye in the building was on us. Many friends had been with us in our journey all year long, others were just learning the facts about Matt's year looked over with curiosity. The speaker first went to Andrea and put his hand on her shoulder and talked about her tragic year. He then went to Matt and put his hand on Matt's shoulder and talked about this cross-country runner and band student whose body had been ravaged by mono, then left to fight back. As he talked I could not help but think how Matt had grown during the year. Had I told him last September that he would be the topic of the graduation program he would have blushed and ran away in sheer panic. But, tonight he sat calmly and accepted all of the attention with calm grace. This experience had made Matt, and our family, grow in many ways.

Once the speaker had finished I began to realize that this was it. It was finally the end of the year we had waited for. I began nervously shaking my legs, and crossed my arms. I knew the big moment was about to begin. As Janet reached over to hold hands with me I was unable to do so. I was nervous and just barely hanging on. As I watched Josh, he had quit sweating but his face was flushed and he was still coughing. I found a sucker in my jacket pocket and had Janet offer it to him. He accepted the sucker, but did not seem too excited about sucking on it during his graduation. Then the big moment began.

They began calling names in the traditional order with the beginning of the alphabet first. I watched a few of Matt's classmate's walk across the stage but I was so nervous my mind began wondering, and panic began setting in. By now Matt had been sitting here for nearly two hours. There had been the band playing, the communion service typical of a Catholic graduation, the ceremony and now the walk across the stage. In therapy Matt had always warmed up, lifted weights, biked and then walked. He had never sat for two hours then gotten out of his chair. I was beginning to have my doubts that he was going to be able to do it. I could not imagine the pressure he was feeling. Walking across the stage was nerve wracking enough, but with crutches for the first time had to create an incredible amount of pressure on him. Then in typical Matt fashion, I knew he would also be concerned about the flipping of the tassel and where he would put his diploma. In his usual fashion, if he was going to do it, it had to be done right.

As they got closer to his name, I grew more and more nervous. Janet had handed the video camera to Andrew and he was shooting the back of a lot of people's heads. Chris and grandma Goge were beginning to fidget, as they wanted to make sure they were in good position to see Matt. Then like a scene from a movie, it was obvious something

Graduating With Honor(s)

was about to happen. Suddenly a big rush of people came down the aisle. The cameramen from the television station and the newspaper led the charge, and behind them were fifteen or twenty other people with cameras. The aisle was now jammed with people. Then, as I saw Josh begin to make his way out of his aisle, I went to him and swelled up for first time. I said, "Josh, carry him if you have to, literally pick him up and carry him, but make sure he gets across the stage!"

Then in the middle of all of the names being called out, the auditorium went completely silent. You could literally hear a pin drop as they called out, "Matthew Daniel Deal." The place was deathly silent. A few nervous coughs, but not a whisper of sound otherwise. I heard some rustling up front, but I could not look up. I sat there with my face in my hands, looking at the floor. I could not look up. I did not want to look up. Janet had long gone to join the throng of picture takers, but I was transfixed in my spot. The whole year was rushing through my head. Then out of the silence it began. Luke Loving yelled in the din "Yeah Matt!" A few other cheers followed that by his classmates, then some cat whistles. Then Matt's senior class rose as one and slowly a standing ovation began. First the students, then the parents, and slowly but surely everyone rose and applauded as Matt made his way across the stage with Josh and Jason. The principals pushed for Josh to hold Matt and help him, but like so many times during the year, Josh just seemed to know Matt was fine, he would make it, and there was no reason to help him now. He was o.k. While the standing ovation continued everyone stood and cheered. While everyone was cheering my son on, I sat with my face in my hands and cried. I cried and cried. I deserved it. We had been strong enough, just long enough. I deserved to enjoy the moment, and to let the anxiety of the past months pass. He was fine, he was making it, and like so many times during the past year, he was in good hands, they could take care of him. I was not needed.

My view of Matt's grand walk was obviously quite limited. Actually it was limited to a piece of the floor about two feet by two feet. I learned later through pictures and the television that as he walked across the stage Andrea had pushed her way through the crowd to give him a hug as he climbed down the stairs. The bishop was in tears as he handed Matt his diploma, and by the end of the steps Matt was shaking and barely able to stand. He had made it, barely, but he had made it!

Not only was this a big step for him, but it was also a big step for a lot of people there. He had been an inspiration to a lot of people, and thank God, he made it! This was the biggest step in Matt's recovery, and he had made it! I felt a million pounds lift from my shoulders.

After Matt finished walking across the stage I sat back and enjoyed the rest of the ceremony. I was proud to watch his friends walk across the stage; kids he had been friends with since kindergarten and elementary school, Danny English, Luke Loving, Kelly O'Shea, Sara Lipeseky, Emily Herdina, Jason Anglin, Dave Frietag and Josh. Then just as I settled in tears began to come to my eyes again as they moved closer to Andrea Wilson's name. Andrea's boyfriend, Matt West, had already gone through the line with the boys. As they neared her name he walked across the aisle, and began pushing Andrea in her wheelchair. Just like

Matt's friends had been there for him, Andrea's were there for her. As Matt West pushed her to the front of the stage the applause began again. He wheeled her onto the stage, then at the point that he was to turn around and go back to the ramp he proceeded to the stairs. There, he picked Andrea up in her wheelchair and carried her down the stairs. Andrea too, had gone across the stage with the rest of her class!

As the graduation winded down there were more tears and hugs. I could not wait to get to Matt and congratulate him. It was just one of those times I wanted to be with him at his side. Janet found him first and was busy taking pictures. He was pretty calm and collected about the whole thing. He acted like that was the way it was supposed to be, and made no big deal about it. It was at that point, watching him that I realized he was definitely not the same son I had run with last summer. He had grown immensely, in many ways. He was not physically the person he had been, but his personality and character had grown beyond what we had ever dreamed. He had truly become a young man of character.

Like most high schools, an all night party follows O'Gorman's graduation. Janet and I had never been real active in attending events with Matt. He had always more or less indicated he wanted to be alone, and did not want us around when he was with his friends. As we left the graduation, we went home and quickly changed. On our way to drop Matt off at the party he asked if we would stay. He thought it would be a good idea if we stayed in case he got tired and needed to come home early. By now he had already been up more than he had been up in nearly nine months, and we had to believe he was getting exhausted.

The party was filled with games, cards, pool tables and a variety of prize drawings, entertainment and food. Matt seemed to enjoy cruising around watching everything and just hanging out. At about midnight the news crew showed up and began following him around. They shot more video for their story, and began interviewing several of his friends. As they followed him into the wee hours of the morning, Matt finally had had enough and politely asked them to quit. He had been a star long enough. He just wanted to just slip back into the role of shy Matt.

As the night slipped to one o'clock, then two o'clock we were a little surprised that Matt still wanted us there. It was obvious he did not need us. His friends were once again taking care of him. As I watched Matt he was still receiving a great deal of attention, but he seemed comfortable with it. At one point during the night he and Andrea found a place in the middle of the room and just sat and talked for a long time. They had never been friends, but through the course of the semester it was obvious a bond had grown between the two. While they had never talked a great deal before, it was obvious as they chatted now, that they did in fact have a great deal in common.

The night slowly began moving toward the morning hours, and I was surprised that Matt, Janet and I were still hanging in there. The adrenaline rush of the day was still hanging with us. As the night began to draw to a close I began to feel sad. I realized that despite the horrific year we had had, we would never feel so loved and so cared for as we had this last year. If bad things were to happen, we were one of the luckiest families in the world that they had happened here. This had been a school community that had really taken care of us. Just how much I don't think we will ever really know.

At 4:00 am the last of the evenings events was to occur in the school auditorium. The senior party was to close with a hypnotist and a showing of the senior class video. As we watched the hypnotist we could not help but to wish for the year back. The opportunity to be able to relive some of the year, to enjoy some of the students and moments of the year more fully. We had missed a great deal, and it was a bittersweet moment watching it come to an end. As the senior video began it was filled with laughs, tears, highs and lows from the senior year. The video ended with what was the highlight of the senior class of 2003 year. The video ended with Matt Deal walking across the stage and graduating with honor! He had made it!

Daniel D. Deal

Happy Birthday Matt

Jessie Tschetter with Matt's Cake

The Birthday Crowd Gathers

A Birthday Kiss

Graduating With Honor(s)

Happy Birthday to you…..

Mr. Smith (Smitty)

The Benefit

Susan Heerts, Janet, Karen Dole

Laurel O'Shea, Lee Ann Sawyer

Ann Tschetter Leads

The Benefit Prayer

Daniel D. Deal

Matt and the Graduating Cousins

Trista, Noelle, Halie

Matt Walking with Cousin Mike at Easter

Dad, Matt, & Mom

Chris, Matt and Andrew

Graduating With Honor(s)

Dave Frietag, Josh Tschetter, Jason Anglin, Jessie Madsen, and Matt

Bishop Carlson, Matt and Josh

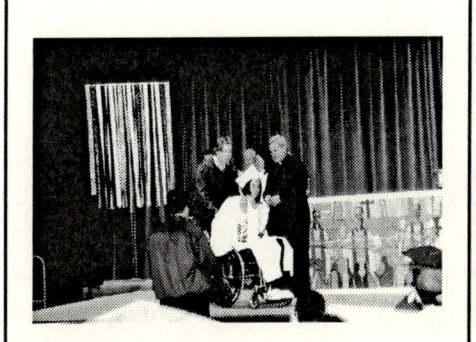

Matt West, Andrea Wilson, Bishop Carlson

Matt & Mom

Daniel D. Deal

The Walk – Josh, Jason, Matt, Dave

Its Done Josh, Matt, Jason, Dave

Josh and Jason

Andrea and Matt

Graduating With Honor(s)

THANK YOU

ANN AND LYNN TSCHETTER

GRADUATING WITH HONOR

Written by:

Dan Deal

1800 W. 39th St.

Sioux Falls, SD 57105

(605) 339-1998 e-mail dandeal@hotmail.com

From Matt

Thanks for all the help and support. It has been incredible and taught me the true meaning of friendship. You have motivated me to continue facing lifes challenges and experience all that it has to offer. Thanks for everything. You inspire me to push on and are true friends. You have been great. Thanks,

Matt Deal

Daniel D. Deal

ABOUT THE AUTHOR

Dan Deal is the father of three young sons, Matthew, Christopher and Andrew. He and his wife Janet have been married for twenty-five years. He began this story in the waiting room of the Mayo Clinic as a chronicle of his son's struggles with an autoimmune disorder that ravaged his nervous system after a bout with mononucleosis. Dan writes about his son Matt's courage and about his friends and a community that gave their family the courage to go on. This story is about the courage all of us have to overcome life's obstacles on step at a time.